Rainbows & Promises

Fifty-two readings from the Bible with
selections from well-loved hymns

Jean Wild

© Day One Publications 2007
First printed 2007

ISBN 978–1–84625–098–9

Unless otherwise indicated, Scripture quotations are from the **New King James Version (NKJV)®**. Copyright © 1982 by Thomas Nelson, Inc. Used by permission. All rights reserved.

All hymns, unless stated otherwise, are taken from
The Redemption Hymnal, Victory Press, 1955.

British Library Cataloguing in Publication Data available

Published by Day One Publications
Ryelands Road, Leominster, HR6 8NZ
☎ 01568 613 740 FAX 01568 611 473
email—sales@dayone.co.uk
web site—www.dayone.co.uk
North American—e-mail—sales@dayonebookstore.com
North American—web site—www.dayonebookstore.com

Cover design by Wayner McMaster

This book came to me at just the right moment—a month after I turned 65! How great are the reminders Jean gives us for the 'third age' of our lives—to ask the Lord to 'speak in the stillness', to remember that 'God holds the key of all unknown', that 'Jesus knows our every weakness', that we are to continue to 'run the straight race', that 'When morning gilds the skies' we can say 'May Jesus Christ be praised'.

John Goldingay, Professor of Old Testament, Fuller Theological Seminary, and Associate Rector, St Barnabas Church, Pasadena

Jean Wild is one of God's ordinary people. Through many years of walking with God she has experienced high and low points. In every circumstance there has been a cheerful smile and a word of encouragement for others. Her faith has been sustained by the Bible and a love of traditional hymns. This book is for similar ordinary people, looking for words of encouragement, hope and inspiration, through all the changing scenes of life.

Declan Flanagan, Chief Executive of Rural Ministries and Chairman of Barnabas Adventure Centres

Jean shares the timeless truths from the good old hymns, in an encouraging and uplifting manner. Many seniors will be particularly blessed as they recall 'bygone days'.

John Townley, Senior Pastor, Light and Life Free Methodist Church, Cornwall

"This book is packed full with rich gospel treasure. My heart was warmed by this thoughtful display of Jesus, our glorious Lord and Saviour. My daily quiet times have always included my old Methodist hymn book, and it is so helpful to find a resource that guides us into the deep waters of the great Christian hymns. In these meditations you will be reminded time and again that in life or death, Jesus is our only hope and comfort."

Rev. Dr Paul Blackham, All Souls Langham Place, London.

Come for a stroll and a chat down 'Memory Lane' and find rainbows of blessing and promises of encouragement along the way. We'll rediscover plenty of memories of days long gone, some to bring smiles and some, maybe, a few tears. All, however, can bring an insight into the special love, care and concern that God has for each of his 'children' of fifty-plus years. So, leaving any regrets behind, let's head towards the everlasting adventure that's waiting for all who are willing to go arm in arm together. Won't you join us as we travel along the pathway that leads to the golden future waiting beyond the sunset?

Dedication

I dedicate this book to Edwin Charles Goldsworthy. For thirty years he was my shepherd, teacher, encourager, and also my friend. My life has been made richer from the times spent with Edwin and Queenie his wife. Their home, and example, was so often a place of comfort for me.

Edwin loved the Bible he also loved to sing these lovely old hymns in his rich tenor voice. Most of all he loved God, which was evident to all by his daily life. Edwin was called to his heavenly home in May 2007. I am happy to know that 'one day' we shall meet again.

Contents

1. Holding hands

Hold thou my hand! so weak I am, and helpless;
I dare not take one step without thy aid!
Hold thou my hand! for then, O loving Saviour,
No dread of ill shall make my soul afraid.

As we stand at the gate of the year

'I said to the man who stood at the gate of the year, "Give me a light, that I may tread safely into the unknown", and he replied, "Go into the darkness and put your hand into the hand of God: that shall be to you better than light and safer than a known way."'

Does that sound familiar? It was quoted in King George VI's Christmas broadcast to the nation in 1939.[1]

Hold hands with the King of kings!

A child will feel safe with his or her small hand in the strong hand of a parent. A parent will hold on to a child in order to protect and guide. When we reach up our hand for help, the Lord is always waiting eagerly to grasp it. Age doesn't matter, and whether it's the hundredth time or the first, he alone is the one we can reach out to. 'Let us therefore come boldly to the throne of grace, that we may ... find grace to help in time of need' (Hebrews 4:16). King George VI called upon God when the nation was at war! What are your needs right now? What does the future hold? We have no idea. But God does! How we need the Lord to be with us individually, by our side, day and night, throughout the coming year.

A mighty, saving hand

Maybe today will be the first time you call out to the Lord for help. He is always waiting for us to call, always waiting to receive us, to forgive our sins, and give us a completely new start, with a glorious eternal life with him in the future. It's not too late for anyone. The Bible assures us, 'Behold, the LORD's hand is not shortened, that it cannot save' (Isaiah 59:1).

Whatever your situation, nothing is impossible for him. No sin is so great that he cannot forgive it. Reach for his hand today.

Bible reading
Psalm 86

Prayer—Never let me go
Heavenly Father, I come to you through our Lord Jesus Christ. I come humbly, as a child with all my needs. I thank you that the hand of the Saviour is always reaching out to me. Forgive me for the times I let go of your hand. Thank you that you never let go. Lift me when I fall; forgive me when I fail; and please hold me tight through the coming year. Amen.

Note

1. Quote from 'The gate of the year' broadcast. Poem by **Minnie Louise Haskins,** 1908.

2. I need thee

I need thee ev'ry hour,
Most gracious Lord;
No tender voice like thine
Can peace afford.
I need thee, oh, I need thee,
Ev'ry hour I need thee;
Oh, bless me now, my Saviour,
I come to thee!

I once asked a dear old friend at the end of her ninety-sixth year, 'What would you like to read in your devotional readings next year?'

Ev'ry hour I need thee

She replied, 'Well, I'd like to be reassured of the Lord's presence and his companionship. I need to know that God cares about me. I would like him to speak into my heart and not just my mind. I want to think the thoughts he wants me to think; to be assured of the Holy Spirit's presence with me all the time. I love the old gospel song that says, "And he walks with me and he talks with me and he tells me I am his own."'

She speaks for so many, doesn't she?

Bless me now, my Saviour

We all need to know these things. She's asking for the Trinity to be with her: Father, Son and Holy Spirit! Can this be possible? Can she have the Father's reassurance that he cares for her? Is it possible for the Son to walk and talk with her? Can she be made aware of it? Can the Holy Spirit within her make these things a reality? When we read the lovely prayer that Jesus prayed to the Father for his disciples, we see that it is indeed possible. How he loves us! We were all on his heart just before he went to the cross to die for us.

No tender voice like thine can peace afford

These were the words that came from his heart, spoken to the heart of the Father for his disciples: 'I in them, and you in me; that they may be made perfect in one, and that the world may know that you have sent me, and have loved them as you have loved me' (John 17:23). Jesus wanted his disciples to know not just how close he was to them, but that he was in them! And not only the twelve disciples; Jesus had already prayed, 'I do not pray for these alone, but also for those who will believe in me through their word' (v. 20). That's us—if we are his disciples also!

Bible reading
John 17

I come to thee—Prayer
Dear heavenly Father, thank you that because you love the Son, you love us also. Thank you that you always hear and answer his prayers. Thank you that he ever lives to pray on our behalf. Amen.

3. Singing stars

The spacious firmament on high,
With all the blue ethereal sky,
And spangled heavens, a shining frame,
Their great Original proclaim.

The heavens declare the glory of God
Have you heard about 'star sales'? Apparently, you may purchase a star, either for yourself or as a gift, and you may give the star the name of your choice. This idea is not a new one! Psalm 147 verses 3 to 4 tell us that our God '… heals the brokenhearted and binds up their wounds. He counts the number of the stars; he calls them all by name.'

Our bright, morning star
So often, in his Word, God loves to tell of his tender love for us, while, at the same time, giving us information about his almighty creative power and glory. The reason for this is that he doesn't want us to be so much in awe of him that we dare not draw near his presence. God has already provided the way to himself through Jesus Christ our Saviour.

Trust the star creator
When Job was experiencing tremendous difficulties, God taught him, in spite of his suffering, not to demand explanations for things he could not, and would never, understand. God asked him a question, to help him view his life and sorrows from God's perspective of eternity: to help him, and us, see our small lives as they really are. 'Where were you when I was creating?' he asks, 'When the morning stars sang together…?' (Job 38:7).

A great Bible understatement!
Genesis 1:16 says 'He made the stars also'! Imagine our scientists giving a news story to the press that they had 'made' one star! What a hullabaloo that would generate! The reports in the media worldwide would run and run. It's certain it wouldn't be announced in an understated five-word sentence! The scientists haven't even *found* all the stars, which isn't

surprising really, as the Bible tells us they are innumerable! Only God knows how many there are. On one occasion, in order to reassure Abram of his everlasting promises, God took him outside to look up at the starry sky (Genesis 15:1–6).

Look up
God loves his creation; he uses it to speak about himself to us. He tells us that, if we were never able to hear or read about him, we would discover what he is like from creation. However, he doesn't want us to worship the creation, but to worship him alone (Deuteronomy 4:19).

Bible reading
Job 38

Prayer
Heavenly Father, we look up at the sky on a starry night and are filled with wonder that you who made the stars and named them, know our names also, and love us. Thank you. Amen.

4. Happy birthday!

More about Jesus would I know,
More of his grace to others show;
More of his saving fulness see,
More of his love who died for me.

More about Jesus let me learn,
More of his holy will discern;
Spirit of God, my teacher be,
Showing the things of Christ to me.

'It's my birthday today, Lord,' I said, half awake one morning. In my heart's 'hearing place' it was as if he replied, 'Yes, I know, I hadn't forgotten: Happy birthday!' 'Oh, I know you never forget anything, Lord; I just mentioned it because it's that special one you spoke of in your Word, the threescore years and ten one, and I must admit I wasn't looking forward to it!' I lay there waiting for a reply, but … nothing! 'Well,' I thought, 'it's no good lying here feeling sorry for myself. I'd better get up.'

Spirit of God, my teacher be
Later, I looked into God's Word. My reading was Psalm 90, which didn't cheer me up at all until I reached verse 12: 'So teach us to number our days, that we may gain a heart of wisdom', and verse 17: 'And let the beauty of the LORD our God be upon us, and establish the work of our hands for us …' Now this I found both helpful and encouraging.

Is beauty only skin deep?
Although we ladies do the best we can with moisturizing face cream, I see that our primary need is for the Lord's beauty to be recognized in us. What a challenge, especially with fewer years ahead than behind! Surely this beauty should have been growing and forming in us gradually over the years?

More of his grace to others show

There's a lovely chorus that says,

Let the beauty of Jesus be seen in me,
All his wondrous compassion and purity,
Oh, thou, Spirit divine, all my nature refine,
Till the beauty of Jesus be seen in me.[2]

How we need his help for *continuing* growth to become more like him day by day and year by year. Is this what is meant by 'growing old gracefully'?

Before I said my bedtime prayers on my birthday night, I asked, 'Lord, I wonder how many years I have left?' Did I only imagine the answer? 'Mind your own business and leave that to me; your times are in my hand!'

Bible reading

Psalm 90

Prayer

Father, help me to grow old gracefully for you, showing your beauty and love to others. Please may I be always willing to obey, believing that whatever you call me to do, you will give me the strength to do it—willingly! Amen.

Note

1. 'Let the beauty of Jesus be seen in me', **Albert Orsborn,** no. 410 in *Mission Praise* (Marshall Pickering, 1990).

5. Planning for the future

Jerusalem, my happy home,
Name ever dear to me!
When shall my labours have an end,
In joy, and peace and thee?
When shall these eyes thy heav'n-built walls
And pearly gates behold?
Thy bulwarks with salvation strong,
And streets of shining gold?

For many years in our town there has been much talk of redevelopment. There have been hours of discussion between architects, planners, builders and backers and, of course, the council! Much talk, but no action. But at last it seems as if things are moving forwards.

By faith we can see it afar!

The local paper now informs us that we should be seeing many changes by 2012! It didn't take me long to realize that I may not be around by then! With that thought came a feeling of disappointment which quite surprised me. As a Christian with faith in Jesus Christ, and totally believing in everlasting life after death for all Christians, I realized what a ridiculous feeling it was. I had to smile at my disappointment, for there is nothing, nothing in this world, that should stop us looking to our eternal destination with anticipation.

A land that is fairer than day!

Living for ever with Jesus and the Father in heaven! Heaven, a place so wonderful that there are no words to describe it! The Bible simply says, 'Eye has not seen, nor ear heard, nor have entered into the heart of man the things which God has prepared for those who love him' (1 Corinthians 2:9). It is not presumptuous for Christians to say this; it is simply trusting in the promises of God in his Word, made to all who will accept his Son, the Lord Jesus Christ, as their Saviour. He gave his life in our place, taking the punishment for our sins upon himself as he died on the cross. He has opened up the way for us to receive eternal life. We are told some facts about heaven: there is no more death, sickness, or tears. We will have new and glorious bodies that will never decay. We will be recognizable to others we knew on earth. Our joy will be perfect, not just because we will see loved ones again, but our absolute joy and satisfaction will be because we are dwelling in the glory with the Father, and actually seeing our precious Saviour.

Bible reading
Psalm 90

Prayer
Lord Jesus, it is wonderful to have the security of knowing that, because of you, one day we will dwell eternally in the presence of our heavenly Father, and see you face to face. Thank you that, by your death and resurrection, you opened up the way to heaven for us. Without forgiveness, we could never enter that perfect place. We dare not live any longer, or die, without you. Amen.

6. Stop and consider!

Speak, Lord, in thy stillness,
While I wait on thee;
Hushed my heart to listen
In expectancy.

Shh, hush, quiet!
Have you ever watched two competitors on TV playing in the chess World Championships? They spend ages deciding which move to make, and can't afford to make a mistake.

But life is so busy nowadays, and not just for the young. We hear retired people saying, 'How did I find time to go to work?' Given that we have the privilege of time, may we choose to spend it in special times with God.

Speak Lord, in thy *stillness*
The Holy Spirit can speak anywhere, anytime, but doesn't often interrupt busy, stressful thoughts. Rather, he speaks in 'a still small voice', and not amid turmoil (1 Kings 19:12).

In this *quiet* hour
He wants our full attention; he knows that when we pray, it isn't always a two-way conversation! After praying, he wants us to stop to listen for his replies. He wants to spend the day with us, but how often does that happen? Remember the Mary and Martha story? 'Martha, Martha, you are worried and troubled about many things. But one thing is needed, and Mary has chosen that good part, which will not be taken away from her' (Luke 10:41–42).

Consider, and don't be anxious
Here are some things to consider quietly: 'the lilies of the field' (Matthew 6:28); 'the birds of the air' (Matthew 6:26); the Saviour (Hebrews 12:2–3).

Jesus, while teaching about provision, used the words 'look at'—look at the flowers and the birds. He doesn't mean 'glance at', but 'learn from'. As our maker, his provision and concern are not only for our material needs;

he is concerned that we have a healthy body, soul and spirit.

Consider creation with your heavenly companion
Stop long enough to smell the roses; don't they give you pleasure, and make you thankful? Discover the hedgerows; did you learn something new? Watch the bird's daily behaviour. Experts tell us the blackbird has a repertoire of between twenty-two and forty-eight songs! Listen quietly, while they sing just for you. In the countryside, enjoy scenery and sky. By the coast, get life in perspective—see the vastness and power of the sea.

Finally, consider Jesus, who loved us so much
'For consider him, who endured such hostility from sinners against himself [for us], lest you become weary and discouraged in your souls' (Hebrews 12:3).

O the deep, deep love of Jesus,
Vast, unmeasured, boundless, free!
Rolling as a mighty ocean
In its fulness over me.

Bible reading
Matthew 6:26–34

Prayer
Please, Lord, remind me every day that I can consider all things with you beside me. Thank you. Amen.

7. The key to the unknown

God holds the key of all unknown,
And I am glad:
If other hands should hold the key,
Or if he trusted it to me,
I might be sad.

God holds the key

There is an amusing cartoon showing a man walking along the pavement, where, just behind him, a window cleaner has just dropped a can full of paint from his ladder! It has missed the man's head by a whisker, but he, whistling happily on his way, is totally unaware of what has just happened behind him!

We aren't always aware of how much God cares for us: what he has kept us from, or what he has kept from us! The next time your programme is interrupted, you miss the bus, or are delayed unexpectedly, remember that cartoon. What seems annoying, when you are in a hurry and something causes a delay, also means you will be in a slightly different place, at a slightly different time!

Be glad that you don't 'hold the key'

Think of bigger problems: hospital appointments or operations suddenly changed at the last minute. Remember, at times like these your heavenly Father is still caring for you, behind the scenes. After your initial disappointment, think: could this be God's arrangement? Maybe a different hospital? A different surgeon? Or even a different outcome? Trust him! 'And we *know* that all things work together for *good* to those who love God, to those who are the called according to his purpose' (Romans 8:28). This means you, if you put your faith and trust in him.

A bird's-eye view

Our way of looking at things is very different from how our Father in heaven sees things from his vantage point. God sees, at a glance, our past, present and future. He not only *sees* all things, he also *knows* all things, so be glad: you can trust him. Being aware of this helps us to understand why God doesn't always answer our prayers in the way we would choose.

He is never unfair; he just knows more!

My will is best

What if tomorrow's cares were here
Without its rest?
I'd rather he unlocked the day,
And, as the hours swing open, say,
'My will is best.'

Don't you think it best that we don't know what the future has in store for us? Can you live the rest of your life trusting in his will for you?

Bible reading
John 1:29–51

Prayer
Let the following be your prayer of faith:

I cannot read his future plans;
But this I know:
I have the smiling of his face,
And all the refuge of his grace,
While here below.

Amen.

8. Our rock, our refuge, our strong tower

Oh, safe to the Rock that is higher than I,
My soul in its conflicts and sorrows would fly.
So sinful, so weary, thine, thine would I be;
Thou blest 'Rock of Ages', I'm hiding in thee.

Landmarks

Most people have a landmark—a local tower, steeple, cross or building—that has become an integral part of the skyline of their home town. A soldier returning on leave to his home town by train said, 'As I looked through the window, I knew the very spot where the rail track curved, and the tower first came into view.'

Safe home

'That moment,' he said, 'I knew I was home. The horror of past months moved away from the front to the back of my mind. Something happened to my heart on seeing that familiar skyline; I felt safe again.' That same edifice will one day crumble and fall down, as have many old monasteries and churches already. Man, unlike God, does not create anything eternal.

Refuge

In Old Testament times, when battles were being fought, 'cities of refuge' were built; within the walls were strong towers, fortresses. People could gather inside them in safety, away from the enemy. King David probably took refuge there. He often prayed and wrote in picture language, trying to convey exactly what he wanted to say. He reassured his own heart with this prayer of affirmation: 'The LORD is my rock and my fortress and my deliverer; my God, my strength, in whom I will trust; my shield and the horn of my salvation, my stronghold. I will call upon the LORD, who is worthy to be praised; So shall I be saved from my enemies' (Psalm 18:2–3).

Hiding in thee

Often, when David was hiding with his soldiers from armies too numerous for them to fight in their own strength, he would call upon the One he could rely on to renew his strength; the One he knew he could trust to come to his aid. 'Deliver me in your righteousness, and cause me to escape; Incline your ear to me, and save me ... For you are my rock and my fortress' (Psalm 71:2–3).

If a warrior king like David found it necessary to call upon the Lord for deliverance and help in times of trouble, surely we should do the same. For he invites us, 'Call upon me in the day of trouble; I will deliver you, and you shall glorify me' (Psalm 50:15).

Bible reading

Psalm 31

Prayer

Father, I come to you in my weakness, believing that, at times, only you can help me. So I run to you, for you are my Rock and hiding place. Amen.

9. Nearer, still nearer

Nearer, still nearer, close to thy heart,
Draw me, my Saviour, so precious thou art;
Fold me, O fold me close to thy breast,
Shelter me safe in that 'Haven of Rest'.

The 'cold shoulder'

At a party or at church, has anyone ever made a beeline for you, and then enveloped you in a big hug with a kiss, when you didn't really want it? Perhaps this happened to the person who coined the expression 'keeping someone at arm's length'! Have you noticed how, as your grandchildren reach eleven or twelve years of age, the kisses and cuddles they once enjoyed are no longer welcome—especially if their friends are around? That's when we can get the 'cold shoulder' and feel sad; we are no longer as close as we once were.

Sadly, without realizing it, we sometimes keep the Lord Jesus 'at arm's length'. We don't draw as close to him as he would like us to be. The Bible shows us this in the many stories where Jesus uses picture language that even a child can understand.

Get the picture?

'How often I wanted to gather your children together, as a hen gathers her chicks under her wings, but you were not willing!' (Matthew 23:37). Maybe the problem is that we feel too 'unworthy' to be too close. But Jesus is the one who makes us worthy: the Father accepts us through him. 'Yet it pleased the LORD to bruise him; he has put him to grief. When you make his soul an offering for sin … he shall see the labour of his soul, and be satisfied' (Isaiah 53:10–11). If the Father is satisfied with Christ's sacrifice, surely we must take advantage of his many invitations to draw close to him—and remain close.

Closer than breathing

His Word tells us, 'in him we live and move and have our being' (Acts 17:28). Sometimes through the day, wherever we are, whatever we may be doing, we should remind ourselves how close he is to us. Have you ever noticed your own heartbeat? Or your lungs breathing in and out, maybe even puffing a little, especially after some exertion? (We're just not as fit as we were!) These occasions can make us more aware of our total dependence upon God.

Bible reading
Isaiah 53

Prayer
Father, I am totally dependant on you. Thank you for the measure of health and strength you give to me each day. Lord Jesus, thank you that you made a way for me to be 'gathered' closely in your arms. Amen.

10. Hidden treasure

Oh, wonderful, wonderful Word of the Lord!
True wisdom its pages unfold:
And though we may read them a thousand times o'er,
They never, no, never grow old.
Each line hath a treasure, each promise a pearl,
That all if we will may secure;
And we know that when time and the world pass away,
God's Word shall for ever endure.

Learn *by* heart, *in* heart

'Your word I have hidden in my heart, that I might not sin against you,' says the psalmist (Psalm 119:11). Do you recall your maths lessons, and the children's sing-song voices, reciting times tables? 'One six is six, two sixes are twelve, three sixes are eighteen', etc. It all seemed so dreary at the time, as we looked out at the sunshine through the window, and waited for playtime. No calculators then to make it easy. Can you still repeat any? Many are still able to do mental arithmetic, referring back to what was learnt, and finding answers now. How grateful we are for our long-term memories. (We won't mention the short-term one! You know! We go from one room to another, and in those few seconds, we've forgotten why we went there!)

Provision in every situation

King David experienced much trouble in his life. He was kept through many dangers, with many battles, many enemies, and many betrayals. He fell into sin, despite God's great blessings to him. Yet he knew and loved the word of God, and was so familiar with it that, in whatever situation he found himself, God's word was instantly there in his mind, available for forgiveness, guidance, wisdom, peace, security and reassurance. Many people think that David was the author of Psalm 119, the longest psalm in the Bible and one in which homage is paid to the word of God. It contains so many references to dependence on God's word. If God's word was so important to King David, it surely ought to be as important to us as our daily food.

Wonderful Word of the Lord

Our Lord Jesus, in the New Testament, depended on God's word! He quotes his Father's words from the Old Testament (Deuteronomy 8:3): 'Man shall not live by bread alone, but by every word that proceeds from the mouth of God' (Matthew 4:4). We, too, can read God's words in the Bible.

Bible reading

Psalm 119:1–48

Prayer

Dear Father of our Saviour the Lord Jesus Christ—the One who lived his perfect life through willing obedience to your word; who made your word alive to us; who showed us how to live depending on your word. Thank you also for the words of your servant David, who, like us a sinner, found your word his sustenance in every situation. Help us to do the same, 'hiding your words in our heart'. Amen.

11. Who will all our sorrows share?

What a friend we have in Jesus, all our sins and griefs to bear;
What a privilege to carry ev'rything to God in prayer.
Oh, what peace we often forfeit, oh, what needless pain we bear—
All because we do not carry ev'rything to God in prayer.

Jesus knows our every weakness

The weeks in the UK before the clocks go forward can seem depressing, especially for those who can't go out much. Days can be gloomy, looking out at a dreary, colourless garden, watching as the rain clouds roll along, listening as the rain beats against the windows. This makes us long for springtime. Have you ever watched as raindrops roll down the windowpane? If you are sad already, it can be a picture of how you feel inside. It's as if the sadness, like the rain, will never end. Of course the rain does end, and sometimes sooner than we expected. Out comes the sun once again, and up pop the dancing daffodils!

Take it to the Lord in prayer

It's these gloomy times when our Lord Jesus really wants us to share our thoughts with him; he is the friend who can really understand. He knows that, even as Christians, we will not always be 'on the mountaintop'. He has lived a real life, in the real world, experienced *every* feeling of sorrow, and can identify with all our feelings:

BEREAVED
At a graveside, Jesus wept.

LONELY
When he was arrested, his friends ran away and left him.

BETRAYED
Peter denied knowing him—Jesus understands how you feel.

HOMELESS
He said, 'Foxes have holes, birds have nests, I have nowhere'—he feels our longings.

ANXIOUS
In Gethsemane, he was 'overwhelmed with sorrow and deeply disturbed'—tell him all about it.

NEEDING SUPPORT
His friends fell asleep! He never sleeps, and is constantly praying for you.

WRONGLY ACCUSED
At his trial, many testified against him. Leave all misunderstandings to him.

RIDICULED WHILE IN PAIN
The soldiers struck him, beat him, spat on him, stripped him, and laughed at him. He knows the worst situations imaginable. Let him comfort you.

Are we weak and heavy laden, cumbered with a load of care?
Precious Saviour, still our refuge—take it to the Lord in prayer.
Do thy friends despise, forsake thee? Take it to the Lord in prayer;
In his arms he'll take and shield thee,
Thou wilt find a solace there.

Bible reading
Matthew 26:30–75

Prayer
Lord Jesus, dearest friend, I come within the loving shelter of your arms, while, just like a little child, I tell you now of all my concerns, great and small. I believe you will hear me and answer, as I trust in you, and allow you to comfort me. Amen.

12. That special look

Rock of Ages, cleft for me,
Let me hide myself in thee!
Let the water and the blood,
From thy riven side which flowed,
Be of sin the double cure;
Cleanse me from its guilt and power.

Seeing ourselves

Sometimes sin can surprise us, especially when we have been a Christian for years. We fall, sometimes flat on our faces, and from that position see ourselves as we really are. Previously, we may have thought we had reached some 'level' of maturity, when, quite unexpectedly, the old nature springs up to trap us, and we sin. We are ashamed, feel guilty, and can feel we have let ourselves and, more importantly, let God down. Thankfully, our Saviour doesn't see things quite like that. He just wants us to return to him quickly for forgiveness. Maybe it's a sin we struggle with, one we have to confess over and over again; the Bible describes it as 'the sin which so easily ensnares us' (Hebrews 12:1). Or maybe it's some new, 'surprising' sin we thought could never tempt us.

Knowing ourselves

Interwoven through the events of Jesus' crucifixion is the story of a man who had something to learn about himself. Peter is the disciple with whom we can all identify. Peter declares he will never let Jesus down, he boasts he will be more faithful than all the other disciples, yet just a few hours later, swearing, declares he doesn't even know Jesus. Instantly, Jesus is aware of what has happened, turns, and gives Peter a very special look. A look for him alone. One that makes him instantly recognize, and regret, what he has done. One that causes him to 'weep bitterly'.

Jesus was on his way to the crucifixion, to die for Peter, to die for us, paying for our sins. Jesus has to show us our sin so we realize the cost for him, and so we can turn to him and repent. 'Seek the LORD while he may be found, call upon him while he is near. Let the wicked forsake his way, and the unrighteous man his thoughts; Let him return to the LORD, and he will have mercy on him; And to our God, For he will abundantly pardon (Isaiah 55:6–7).

Forgiveness and restoration

Following the Resurrection, Peter was given a lovely opportunity for forgiveness as Jesus asked, 'Do you love me?' Peter replied, 'Yes Lord; you know that I love you' (John 21:15).

What would you reply in answer to Jesus' question?

Bible reading

John 21:1–25

Prayer

Lord Jesus, help me to return to you quickly when I fall, when you give me that special look, the one that calls me to seek your forgiveness. Amen.

13. Heaven

Golden harps are sounding, angel voices ring,
Pearly gates are opened—opened for the King;
Jesus, King of glory, Jesus, King of love,
Is gone up in triumph to his throne above.
He who came to save us, he who bled and died
Now is crowned with glory at his Father's side.
Nevermore to suffer, nevermore to die;
Jesus, King of glory, is gone up on high.
Praying for his children in that blessèd place;
Calling them to glory, sending them his grace;
His bright home preparing faithful ones for you;
Jesus ever liveth, ever loveth too.

Inside those 'pearly gates'

One day when my son was a teenager, we discussed our thoughts about heaven. We arrived at the following ideas: new colours never seen before; new notes of music never heard before; new flavours and aromas; people travelling through space at the speed of light; and many similar ideas to do with travel (most originating from *Star Trek*!). One that made us laugh was of using fluffy white clouds as trampolines! How foolish we were!

Eyes and ears

It's no use speculating, because we, within the confines of our minds, will always be wrong. The Bible knows our imaginations and says, 'Don't even bother trying to imagine, you will never get it right!' 'But as it is written: "Eye has not seen, nor ear heard, nor have entered into the heart of man the things which God has prepared for those who love him"' (1 Corinthians 2:9). The apostle Paul tells of an 'experience' he had. We know that he was chosen by God to bring the message of salvation to Gentiles. People with very special callings sometimes get special revelations. Paul wasn't a boastful person and speaks about himself this way: 'I know a man in Christ who fourteen years ago … whether in the body or out of the body I do not know, God knows—how he was caught up into Paradise and heard inexpressible words, which it is not lawful for a man to utter' (2 Corinthians 12:2–4). These were amazing mysteries, better than anything seen or heard before and too marvellous to speak of down here.

No more ...
... Sin, sickness, pain or death, sorrow, tears, or parting. That is certainly something to look forward to! Enjoy living now, a day at a time, but there is a wonderful eternal life ahead for those who have replied to Jesus' invitation of salvation.

Bible reading
RSVP: Matthew 22:1–14

Prayer
Lord, as you now hear those 'angel voices', you also hear our sighs, feel our pain, and are aware of every parting. I say now my prayer of faith and trust in you that will ensure a place inside those pearly gates reserved for me. Amen.

14. Leaning

At even, ere the sun was set,
The sick, O Lord, around thee lay;
O in what divers pains they met!
O with what joy they went away!
Once more 'tis eventide and we,
Oppressed with various ills, draw near;
What if thy form we cannot see,
We know and feel that thou art here.

Never felt better!

Many grandparents today are pretty busy, helping out with grandchildren, being as busy and active as ever. 'The children keep us young and on our toes,' they say. Some have even returned to the workplace! Among these folk, you won't see many crimplene dresses or brogues; instead, brightly coloured T-shirts, jeans and trainers! We are told seventy is the new sixty, and eighty is the new seventy! So if we are to believe it, we're getting younger as we live longer!

Some are sick

O Saviour Christ, our woes dispel:
For some are sick, and some are sad,
And some have never loved thee well,
And some have lost the love they had.

Very different are another group we see around us, who suffer from 'various ills'. Perhaps you've noticed those who have to stop and rest while shopping. Or someone leaning on a wall halfway up the hill, pretending to look at the view, but really waiting for the inhaler to work so he or she can continue on their way. Others we notice with obviously arthritic joints, suffering a painful and sometimes disabling disease.

Some are sad

Still others show no outward signs of sickness; they 'suffer in silence', having long discovered that when people ask 'How are you?' they are not interested in hearing the answer! Do they know there is someone who will listen, someone who will understand? This is our Lord Jesus himself. He wants those who are weak in body and in soul to 'lean' on him—draw strength and comfort from him! 'And Jesus went about ... healing all kinds of sickness and all kinds of disease among the people' (Matthew 4:23). Do you think he cares any the less, now he is seated at the right hand of the Father in glory? Jesus is very familiar with the sickroom and the hospital. His presence is constantly in the wards and operating theatres. How many people do you think are wheeled down the corridor to face major surgery without 'calling on the name of the Lord'? Speak to him, for he invites us to 'call upon me in the day of trouble' (Psalm 50:15).

Bible reading
Psalm 86

Prayer
Thy touch has still its ancient power;
No word from thee can fruitless fall;
Hear in this solemn evening hour,
And in thy mercy heal us all.

15. Teach me thy way

Teach me thy way, O Lord,
Teach me thy way!
Thy gracious aid afford,
Teach me thy way!
Help me to walk aright,
More by faith, less by sight;
Lead me with heavenly light:
Teach me thy way!

Long as my life shall last,
Teach me thy way!
Where'er my lot be cast,
Teach me thy way!
Until the race is run,
Until the journey's done,
Until the crown is won,
Teach me thy way!

Do we have all the answers?

We can all think we're pretty smart when we're watching TV quiz shows. We confidently shout out the answers to the *Countdown* contestants. We know that, if we had the chance, we would not be *The weakest link*! When it comes to *University Challenge*, however, we are not quite so ready with the answers! We realize that we are not as clever as we thought. How wise, and intelligent in the subjects they have studied, these young students seem to be!

We hear politicians and TV personalities giving their opinions on major issues affecting the whole of our country; out of their 'worldly wisdom' they spend so much time discussing the nation's many problems. But it's all just words, words, words—and we recognize that there is nothing of God's wisdom in them. The Bible teaches us, 'For the wisdom of this world is foolishness with God' (1 Corinthians 3:19). God in his wisdom sums up our national problems in four short words: 'Righteousness exalts a nation ...'

(Proverbs 14:34). We hear and respect his wisdom in that, and know we need to consult him in everything.

Teach us
'So teach us to number our days, that we may gain a heart of wisdom' (Psalm 90:12). These words are addressed to all, but they do seem all the more meaningful when we have reached the threescore years and ten mark (Psalm 90:10)! It seems we have to be taught by God before it is too late, and we are never too old to learn. It doesn't matter to God how much knowledge, experience or worldly wisdom we have acquired (even Bible 'head knowledge' is not enough!). The wisdom that comes from God has to be received into our hearts and become part of us. He longs to fill our hearts and minds with his wisdom. We have to be a willing participant in opening our hearts, as well as our minds, to his Son, our Saviour the Lord Jesus, in whom dwell all the wisdom and fulness of God (Colossians 1:19; 2:9).

Bible reading
Matthew 25:1–13

Prayer
Father, thank you for giving me the wisdom to accept Jesus into my life today. Amen.

16. What's in a name?

Join all the glorious names
Of wisdom love and power,
That mortals ever knew,
That angels ever bore:
All are too mean to speak his worth,
Too mean to set my Saviour forth.

Names are pretty important aren't they? It's surprising how often we need them. A cat often comes into my garden; I don't know his name, but I call him 'Marmalade'. Well, it's obvious why I chose that name, because he's orange and stripy! Marmalade is what he reminds me of!

We read that God sometimes changed people's names, usually when they were about to do something special for him, or when they had a big change in their lives. Think of Abraham: what a calling! And Simon Peter: what a tremendous change we see in him! How wonderful to know that when we first became Christians, God wrote our name down in a book, and it's there for ever! 'But there shall by no means enter it [heaven] anything that defiles, or causes an abomination or a lie, but only those who are written in the Lamb's Book of Life' (Revelation 21:27). God must have thought that we, as individuals, are important enough to be recorded in heaven! That makes us feel pretty special, doesn't it? I wonder: when our names were first written there, was there a change in us? Are we still changing, and growing spiritually?

All are too mean to speak his worth

God has names for himself that describe his character and attributes. He wants us to know what he is like, and, the more we know about him, the more we will understand that we can trust him with our lives, and, more important still, with our souls, which will live for ever. Jesus has many names that speak of his love and care for us: Shepherd, Friend, Refuge, Prophet, Priest and King. There are many more—it's almost as if there are not enough words to describe him. Each name reveals him in a different role. Every time we come to him in need (and those needs are different for each one of us), he will be to us exactly what we need, for he knows us better than we know ourselves. His names tell us that he is everything and more than we could ever need, and that he can be 'everything' to us.

Name of Jesus! highest Name!
Name that earth and heaven adore!
From the heart of God it came,
Leads me to God's heart once more.

Bible reading
Matthew 1:16–25

Prayer
Dear Lord Jesus, I thank you that you love me in every way. Of all your glorious names, the name I love best is 'Jesus my Saviour'! Amen.

17. I will guide thee

Precious promise God hath given
To the weary passer-by,
On the way from earth to heaven,
'I will guide thee with mine eye.'

'I will guide thee, I will guide thee,
I will guide thee with mine eye;
On the way from earth to heaven,
I will guide thee with mine eye.'

The way from earth to heaven.

Picture a journey from earth to heaven, seeing the universe as the astronomers describe. It seems an impossible distance to travel. It would seem hopeless, unless you are one of the people who have already booked a ticket for 'a journey into space'! Would you really like to put your faith in an uncertain future like that? So, how do we find our way from earth to heaven?

Jesus is the way

John the Baptist said to those who came to hear his preaching, 'Repent, for the kingdom of heaven is at hand' (Matthew 3:2), meaning that the Saviour was coming. When he came onto the scene, Jesus gave a warning to those who were listening to his teaching: Repentance must be followed by a consistent Christian lifestyle! 'For I say to you, that unless your righteousness exceeds the righteousness of the scribes and Pharisees, you will by no means enter the kingdom of heaven' (Matthew 5:20). Later, when explaining to his followers that the kingdom of heaven was not very far away at all, Jesus said something astounding: 'The kingdom of God does not come with observation; nor will they say, "See here!" or "See there!" For indeed, the kingdom of God is within you' (Luke 17:20–21). He was speaking of the personal and very close relationship that must exist between ourselves, the Father, the Son, and the Holy Spirit. Do you realize how close the kingdom is to you? Do you have that close relationship? Do you ask him for guidance?

I will guide thee with mine eye

With his all-seeing eye, God observes our lives from start to finish (Psalm 139). He treats us all individually, as we are all on our own unique journey with him. Is the journey sometimes difficult? Yes! Sometimes it is. When temptations come along, will he help us be strong? Yes! He will if we ask him. When we have losses and disappointments, does he know? Yes! He does know, and shares in them.

When thy secret hopes have perished
In the grave of years gone by,
Let this promise still be cherished,
'I will guide thee with mine eye.'

Bible reading

Psalm 139

Prayer

Dear Father God, thank you for the Saviour who opens the way to heaven for us, and who brings the kingdom even within us. Please guide me all the days of my life. Amen.

18. The heart of God

There is a place of quiet rest,
Near to the heart of God;
A place where sin cannot molest,
Near to the heart of God.

O Jesus, blest Redeemer,
Sent from the heart of God;
Hold us, who wait before thee,
Near to the heart of God.

There is a place of comfort sweet,
Near to the heart of God;
A place where we our Saviour meet,
Near to the heart of God.

There is a place of full release,
Near to the heart of God;
A place where all is joy and peace,
Near to the heart of God.

The mind of God
It's very likely that, by now, we have realized we shall never understand the
mind of God. Like Paul, we admit our human minds could never contain
his knowledge:
'Oh, the depth of the riches both of the wisdom and knowledge of God!
How unsearchable are his judgements and his ways past finding out!'
(Romans 11:33).

Past finding out
So we accept we could spend a lifetime trying to understand all God's
dealings with us. Sometimes he graciously gives us a 'little peep' of insight
into certain matters, usually when we are 'seeking his face', reading his
Word, or praying for his guidance. God just longs for us to know of his

great heart of love towards us. He wants to be near enough to talk with us 'heart to heart'. Throughout the Old Testament the Father's love calls out to Israel in their disobedient wanderings. His heart of love is displayed through words and deeds; provision; guidance; repeated forgiveness, grace and mercy—and no less towards us today!

Jesus, sent from the heart of God

God's mind may be a mystery to us, but his heart need never be! There is a mystery he longs for us to know and accept by faith. He has revealed it to us in his Son: 'To you it has been given to know the mystery of the kingdom of God' (Mark 4:11). The ultimate loving heart, broken yet willing in the giving of his beloved Son; our Saviour, the ultimate example of obedience, hating the thought of being 'made sin for us' (2 Corinthians 5:21). Yet he was still willing to come to bring the gift of salvation, which is for us the entrance to the kingdom of God. 'For God so loved the world that he gave his only begotten Son, that whoever believes in him should not perish but have everlasting life' (John 3:16). God's heart in one verse!

Bible reading

Isaiah 55

Prayer

Whether for the first time, or one of many, draw very near, and have your own 'heart to heart' with God.

19. Will your anchor hold?

Will your anchor hold in the storms of life?
When the clouds unfold their wings of strife;
When the strong tides lift and the cables strain,
Will your anchor drift, or firm remain?

Storms, clouds, strife

What do you think of as you read those words? What do the clouds of strife represent? What makes you feel tossed about, and makes your 'cables strain'? Can you look back on your life, and recognize times when Jesus has been with you in your troubles? Have your life experiences taught you patience and perseverance through trials, when life seemed difficult? Jesus told us when we first committed our lives to him that it wouldn't always be an easy 'sail' through life. He doesn't always explain his ways to us.

The Bible tells us that in this life troubles will come along—Christians are not exempt from them (John 16:33).

An anchor to rely on

God did promise, however, that he would always be alongside to keep us on course. What he wants in return is our obedience and trust, and he expects that, even through the hard times. He will be our firm Anchor. He has promised to hold us safely, keeping us secure, even though we have to lift and strain while enduring the strife.

Mr Noah ...

Do you remember singing this chorus in Sunday School?

Mr Noah built an ark, the people thought it such a lark!
Mr Noah pleaded so, but into the ark they would not go.

Mr Noah certainly experienced storms in his life! He had responsibility for building a massive ark, then the care of Mrs Noah, his family, and all the animals. He could certainly tell us a thing or two about the strain and strife inside the ark! However, he knew and trusted the One who had the responsibility of keeping the ark afloat. You see, Noah had instructions from God, they had an agreement, and Noah was obedient (Genesis 6). An outline for us! We won't have to persevere as long as Noah did, but, inevitably, we will all meet difficulties. We must never despair. 'Blessed be the God and Father of our Lord Jesus Christ, the Father of all mercies and God of all comfort, who comforts us in all our tribulation ...' (2 Corinthians 1:3–4). The Lord has promised to keep us safely within 'the ark' of his care.

We have an anchor that keeps the soul
Steadfast and sure while the billows roll:
Fastened to the Rock which cannot move,
Grounded firm and deep in the Saviour's love!

Bible reading
Genesis 6–7

Prayer
In your own words, make sure you are 'safe'.

20. Did God say 'Retire'?

To the work! to the work! we are servants of God,
 Let us follow the path that our Master has trod;
With the balm of his counsel our strength to renew,
Let us do with our might what our hands find to do.

A fork in the pathway

Birthdays can be quite good times for making reassessments of our lives, especially our spiritual lives. At retirement, it can be as though we are standing at a fork in our pathway. We could look left to the retirement path and think, 'Cups of tea in bed, armchair, slippers and daytime TV.' However, the Bible doesn't talk about retirement—in fact, if you think about the seniors we read about there, God apparently kept them pretty busy! As far as he is concerned, age is no excuse for dropping out. Think of Mr and Mrs Noah, Abraham, Sarah, and Naomi. Think what God accomplished because they were willing! Age was never an issue with God, but *obedience* was!

The right path

If you are one of the many fortunate 'third age' people who are healthy, and still living an active life, instead of only thinking, 'Exercise classes, night school, day trips, gardening, sightseeing, foreign holidays, etc.' (there is enough choice out there to fill every hour of every day!), why not make some time for some of the variety of opportunities for serving the Lord, at church, maybe, or in a different way—perhaps stepping down from 'what you have always done' to make room for the younger generation to take their place. They may not do the work in the same way you did—but remember, we all have to learn; we probably didn't do things in the same way as our elders! Different can be good sometimes! And, sometimes, the Lord may be trying to do 'a new thing' in your church, and a new thing for you! If you can't think of anything yourself, your minister/pastor will know only too well where the needs are, and what you could do to remain a useful, contributing church member. On the other hand, how about serving in some way in your local community? That's one way people will see the church 'in action'—one way of being the 'salt and light' Jesus told us to be.

Bible reading
Matthew 5:1–16

Prayer
Dear Lord, let us not grow weary, or be lazy, once we have retired from our occupations. Show each of us that specific work for you that only we can do. If you choose the work for us, we can then trust that you will enable us to do it. Amen.

21. Abide with me

Abide with me; fast falls the eventide;
The darkness deepens; Lord, with me abide;
When other helpers fail, and comforts flee,
Help of the helpless, O abide with me.

I wonder why they sing 'Abide with me' at the FA cup final? Maybe the fans hope that God will help their side win! Christians sing 'Who is on the Lord's side?' not 'Whose side is the Lord on?' The fans continue to sing out with gusto words that make us wonder whether they realize who they are singing to. We know and love these words, and our Saviour to whom we sing.

Other helpers fail
We know by now that, at certain times, 'other helpers', even our nearest and dearest, won't come up to expectations. How could they? We couldn't come up to theirs, either! The Lord wants us to make *him alone* responsible for meeting all our needs, keeping us joyful, or making our lives complete. Only he can do that. He will never fail us when we come to him. Totally dependable, he assures us in his Word, 'I will never leave you nor forsake you' (Hebrews 13:5).

Who but thyself can foil the tempter's power?
We also know what this means. We have been tried and tested many times through the years. Did we think that, as we grew older, temptations would be fewer, easier to resist, or even leave us alone altogether? No, the daily fight continues, the old nature rises up to remind us it's still there. We can't be complacent either, Paul warns us, before following the warning with the reassurance that God will never allow more temptation into our lives than we can bear. When we ask for help and strength, God will always hear and help us (1 Corinthians 10:12–13).

Help of the helpless
Have you noticed those special worries Satan loves to whisper to us?

Questions about today: 'Why?' Anxieties about the future: 'How?' 'When?' 'Where?' Regrets about the past: 'If only …'—how memories return! The devil can have a heyday if we allow those thoughts to linger. In our thoughts—that is where he attacks, but the battle should be fought and won at the start.

Abide with me

'You will keep him in perfect peace, whose mind is stayed on you, because he trusts in you' (Isaiah 26:3). Can *we* trust him to be with us always?

Bible reading

Psalm 23

Prayer

Father God, when my anxious thoughts arise, quieten my heart and mind; help me feel your presence with me, reminding me that Jesus is already victorious. Help me hand over to you any anxious thoughts that take away your peace from me. Amen.

22. Promises, promises

Standing on the promises of Christ our King,
Through eternal ages let his praises ring:
Glory in the highest, I will shout and sing,
Standing on the promises of God.

Standing on the promises that cannot fail,
When the howling storms of doubt and fear assail
By the living word of God I shall prevail,
Standing on the promises of God.

Promises: broken or eternal?

If you have ever experienced a broken promise, you may still remember the feeling, even from childhood. Parents and friends can make promises they don't keep. A broken promise to a child can seem as hurtful as an adult's broken engagement, or unfaithfulness. However, God doesn't want us to go on carrying the hurt of broken promises, but rather to trust in him, for he has made so many wonderful and eternal promises to us. Let him erase all our past disappointments.

Standing on his promises

God's promises never change. They stand as strong and secure as when he first spoke them. When God speaks, every single word is pure truth. It is impossible for him to lie, or change his mind. He never wastes a word. When he speaks, it happens, has happened, or will most surely happen in the future. We can depend on it (Titus 1:2).

Promises that cannot fail

Our Father's promises come to us today through our Lord Jesus Christ (Hebrews 10:19–23).

Through eternal ages

There is a promise that Christians through the ages have clung to in times of danger, sorrow, doubt and despair—precious words of the Lord, so easy to memorize and keep in our hearts: 'I will never leave you nor forsake you' (Hebrews 13:5).

When doubt and fear assail
If we allow it, it's so easy to feel some anxiety regarding growing old. We hear the horror stories of when 'Care in the Community' and residential homes fail. (The media don't tell us about the majority of good ones!) Do you have concerns about being able to stay in your own home? Having to go into care, or hospital? Maybe even being a 'burden' to your family?

I shall prevail
Our Father knows all about it; trust him who says, '[You] who have been upheld by me from birth, who have been carried from the womb: even to your old age, I am he, and even to grey hairs I will carry you! I have made, and I will bear; Even I will carry, and will deliver you (Isaiah 46:3–4).

Bible reading
Psalm 34

Prayer
Thank you, Father, for all your precious promises to us. Help us to hold them in our hearts. You know our concerns, so we hand them over to you, trusting in your Word. Amen.

23. OAP? God says VIP!

On thee my heart is resting!
Ah, this is rest indeed!
What else, Almighty Saviour,
Can a poor sinner need?
Thy light is all my wisdom,
Thy love is all my stay;
Our Father's home in glory
Draws nearer every day.

When clouds are darkest round me
Thou, Lord, art then most near,
My drooping faith to quicken,
My weary soul to cheer.
Safe nestling in thy bosom,
I gaze upon thy face;
In vain my foes would drive me
From thee, my hiding place.

OAPs

Our group didn't go in the restaurant recommended for the lovely meals they serve. We chose another instead; we simply didn't like the words on the menu board, on the pavement outside. In very large letters, it informed us that 'Old Age Pensioners' could have 'cut-price meals'. The second half of the message seemed very acceptable! It was just the title we had been given. We all agreed that we didn't like it, or the image it gave. No, we weren't denying our age, but we would all prefer to be known as 'senior citizens'. That term sounds more respectful.

Walking down the High Street, anyone aged over fifty seems to become invisible to groups of teenagers as they are jostled aside. We can recall the days when gentlemen raised their hats as we passed by. Children were taught manners and respect. We have accepted now that those days are long gone!

VIPs

We read that God thinks of us not as OAPs, but as VIPs! Yes, he thinks we're a pretty special bunch! He has given us a verse of our very own in Leviticus, where God gives instructions to Moses for the people: 'You shall rise before the grey headed and honour the presence of an old man, and fear your God: I am the LORD' (Leviticus 19:32). Firstly, God showed them their responsibilities towards him, the holy God: the importance of asking for, and receiving, forgiveness for sin before they may worship him acceptably. Secondly, he showed them their responsibilities in regard to their neighbour. In the New Testament, 'the two greatest commandments' are interpreted for us by Jesus: we are to love God with our whole heart, and love our neighbour as ourselves. 'Our' verse in Leviticus is included under the second command.

Bible reading

Matthew 5:1–19

Prayer

Father, we don't want to become 'grumpy old folk'. Please keep us sweet-natured, and not 'touchy'. Help us to keep our sense of humour. Let us bring all that hurts us to you. Help us to behave in such a way that we may earn the respect due to us, according to your Word. Amen.

24. I am the good shepherd

Thine for ever! Lord of love,
Hear us from thy throne above;
Thine for ever may we be,
Here and in eternity.

Thine for ever! Shepherd, keep
These thy frail and trembling sheep;
Safe alone beneath thy care,
Let us all thy goodness share.

'The Lord is my shepherd'

So often we sing Psalm 23 at weddings and funerals. David, the psalmist, didn't intend it for special occasions only. It was to testify of the Lord's care throughout his life. As a boy, after training he became a shepherd himself, so he knew the special bond that existed between the shepherd and each individual sheep. So we have to say, 'My shepherd'. Eastern shepherds don't walk behind their flocks as ours do, but lead from the front while looking out for any strays lagging behind, often with sheepdogs circling around, chasing the wanderers, and nipping their legs to direct them back. The sheep don't like that, but it works! The good shepherd knows each sheep, giving them names according to their characteristics. He hears, and responds to the bleating of each one. Using his crook (staff) he draws them back. He uses his short but extremely heavy truncheon (rod) on any attacker. Perhaps if there are some very disobedient sheep, he gives them a short sharp shock also! At nightfall, however, how glad they are to be back safe within the fold after having been chastised. At night, still on duty, the shepherd lights a large fire outside to scare away dangerous prowling animals, and lies down to rest across the entrance. Nothing can leave or enter without his knowledge. 'I am the door. If anyone enters by me, he will be saved' (John 10:9).

The lost sheep

Sometimes when he knows the flock is safe, he leaves it to go and search for a single lost sheep.

What man of you, having a hundred sheep, if he loses one of them, does not leave the ninety-nine in the wilderness, and go after the one which is lost until he finds it? And when he has found it, he lays it on his shoulders, rejoicing. And when he comes home, he calls together his friends and neighbours, saying to them, 'Rejoice with me, for I have found my sheep which was lost!'… Likewise I say to you, there is joy in the presence of the angels of God over one sinner who repents (Luke 15:4–10).

Bible reading
John 10:1–18

Prayer
Lord Jesus, thank you that we heard you calling us, and for receiving us into your fold and leading us daily. Draw us near when we wander. If we are like the lost sheep, we ask to be received into your fold today, as we trust you to lead us home. Amen.

25. Keeping in touch

I need thee every hour,
Most gracious Lord;
No tender voice like thine
Can peace afford.

I need thee, oh, I need thee,
Ev'ry hour I need thee;
Oh, bless me now, my Saviour,
I come to thee!

I need thee every hour,
Stay thou near by;
Temptations lose their power,
When thou art nigh.

Chatting all day!

We know that God would never ask us to do something impossible. Through our Saviour's death on the cross, he has already done what we never could do for ourselves. Because he loves us, he wants us to experience his presence throughout the day. When we are told to 'pray without ceasing' (1 Thessalonians 5:17), reason tells us that it can't mean staying on our knees 'saying our prayers'; it simply means remaining in close communication with the Lord God every minute of the day, remembering that, as Paul tells us, 'in him we live and move and have our being' (Acts 17:28). Talking with him is an important part of our one-to-one relationship—what a privilege! Our Lord wants to converse with us!

Temptations lose their power if thou art nigh

These thoughts of intimacy can make us feel a little uncomfortable; maybe it's because we realize that we do not always behave in a way that Jesus would find pleasing! Yet perhaps this knowledge could help us to resist temptation—or at least encourage us to keep short accounts with him! We may ask for forgiveness immediately we realize that what we said or did without much thought was not pleasing to him. This means that we share every experience with him, the good and the bad—he knows us through and through already, anyway! He wants us to know how much he takes pleasure in us; he rejoices in our victories and achievements, great and small. He wants to bring his forgiveness quickly to us, not wanting us to experience hours, or days, of guilt, but to lift us up and set us right again. How our bedtime prayers would benefit from a day spent like this!

'Be still and know that I am God'

How often have we spent sleepless hours worrying? He wants us to bring every concern to him as it arises. The next time you lay your head on the pillow, remember: he is the one who never sleeps; he will be awake and in control all night, and already knows how it will all work out in the end! Tell him, lay it down, and leave it with him.

Bible reading

Acts 17:16–34

Prayer

Let your bedtime 'Good night, Lord' be a continuation of the conversation with your daytime companion 'who is able to do exceedingly abundantly above all that we ask or think' (Ephesians 3:20).

26. New every morning

When morning gilds the skies,
My heart awaking cries,
'May Jesus Christ be praised!'

First thoughts

What is the first thought that comes into your mind when you wake up? No! Not 'I must go to the bathroom, quickly'! But as you lie still, resting, as your thoughts begin to stir, and as *you* decide whether to accept or reject the negative worried ones. Does God want you to begin a new day like this? Is this the time for you to worry about what the day has in store? It needn't be, if you remember that God's mercies are constant. At the start of each new day is a good time to remember this.

New every morning

We read in his word, 'His compassions fail not. They are new every morning; Great is your faithfulness. "The LORD is my portion," says my soul, "Therefore I hope in him!"' (Lamentations 3:22–24). Was there a time when your first thoughts were for God alone? Thankful thoughts of your new-found faith in his Son, your Saviour? 'Can it be true that Jesus died for me?' Early-morning thoughts to be relished, as the wonder of forgiveness and spiritual new birth filled your mind. Did they also fill your heart, filling it with praise and amazement that God should offer his love to you—ordinary, sinful, insignificant you? Why? Well, not because you deserved it, that's for sure!

May Jesus Christ be praised

Is it so long ago that you have forgotten these special words? 'For God so loved the world that he gave his only begotten Son, that whoever believes in him should not perish but have everlasting life' (John 3:16). Have you also forgotten that 'whoever' included you, and still does? Your day could turn out to be quite different if you began it with a prayer of wonder, appreciation and praise. Then continue carrying that feeling in your heart throughout each day. The Holy Spirit will remind you, if you will let him.

My heart awaking cries

You may be thinking, 'I never felt like that!' If so, God's 'special offers' of mercy do not have a closing date on them! (Well, after death is too late, of course!) Today could be your day. Why not wake up to a new morning, with a new way of thinking, a new faith, a new outlook on your day—every day! Let this be your prayer today:

Bible reading

1 John 3:16

Prayer

'His compassions fail not. They are new every morning; Great is your faithfulness. "The LORD is my portion," says my soul, "Therefore I hope in him!"' (Lamentations 3:22–24).

27. Still growing

More about Jesus would I know,
More of his grace to others show;
More of his saving fulness see,
More of his love who died for me.

More about Jesus let me learn,
More of his holy will discern;
Spirit of God, my teacher be,
Showing the things of Christ to me.

More about Jesus, in his Word,
Holding communion with my Lord;
Hearing his voice in every line,
Making each faithful saying mine.

Inch by inch

For children, every inch taller means an inch nearer being a 'grown up'. By
twenty, we are fully grown. In our twenties, we sang about having the key to
the door! After our thirties, it seemed to be somewhere around our middle
that the inches grew!

More about Jesus let me learn

No matter how old we are when we become a Christian, God expects us to
continue growing: in faith, in trust, in love for him and others, in knowledge
of him and his Word, and in wisdom. There's quite a bit of growth still
needed, then! Both Peter and Paul, having been taught by the Master,
remind us that we haven't yet reached our spiritual potential. Paul declares,
'Not that I have already attained, or am already perfected; but I press on,
that I may lay hold of that for which Christ Jesus has also laid hold of me'
(Philippians 3:12). Peter tells us we are to 'grow in the grace and knowledge
of our Lord and Saviour Jesus Christ' (2 Peter 3:18). How do we do this?
There is quite a simple answer, for God the Father doesn't make the way of
learning more about Jesus a problem. You may remember a Sunday school

chorus that was simple enough for children and adults to understand: 'Read your Bible, pray every day if you want to grow!' There we have it!

Spirit of God my teacher be

Because of what God has done for us, he has the right to desire more of us, and within this loving relationship he expects us to desire more of him! Paul says similar words to Peter's: 'As you ... have received Christ Jesus the Lord, so walk in him, rooted and built up in him and established in the faith' (Colossians 2:6–7).

Bible reading

John 15

Prayer—holding communion with your Lord

Lord, I could spend so much time looking back, regretting the years I have wasted, and now there seems so little time to grow more in the knowledge of yourself and your Word. Help me now only to look forward towards a wonderful, eternal future, as I continue walking with you, totally dependant on you, listening always as your Word speaks to me, learning, as the Holy Spirit teaches me, more and more about Jesus, hearing his voice in every line. Amen.

28. Homeward bound

All the way my Saviour leads me,
Cheers each winding path I tread,
Gives me faith for every trial,
Feeds me with the Living Bread.
Though my weary steps may falter,
And my soul athirst may be,
Gushing from the Rock before me,
Lo! a spring of joy I see.

All the way my Saviour leads me;
Oh, the fulness of his love!
Perfect rest to me is promised
In my Father's house above.
When my spirit, clothed, immortal,
Wings its flight to realms of day,
This my song through endless ages,
Jesus led me all the way.

All the way

What an undertaking! Peter and Gwen Beckett posed for a photograph under the well-known Land's End signpost in Cornwall, which read, '874 miles. To God be the glory!' They beamed around with great smiles of achievement to their 'Welcoming committee' of relatives and friends, amid balloons and 'Welcome back!' and 'Well done!' banners, to the sound of cheering. At retirement, they had decided they would do this one day, God willing!

Setting off with home in view

After careful discussion and planning they travelled up to Scotland to start the walk, as they wanted to finish the journey at 'home' in Cornwall. From the start, they knew that suitable clothing, with good waterproofs, was essential, along with strong hiking boots. They had some idea of what they were taking on and had planned as far as possible for every eventuality.

My Saviour leads me

Prayerfully, they put themselves in the Lord's hands and under his daily care. In capital letters, at the top of their carefully selected list of requirements, they wrote: 1) The Lord's continual presence; 2) Full commitment in our part; 3) Always keep our destination in view; 4) No regrets or looking back. Finding a room for the night and regular nourishment were also priorities, as were rest and a refreshing shower (oh, the relief of 'Boots off!' and the application of soothing ointment and plasters for blisters). I wonder, does this remind you of our life journey? Can you see how the Christian walk requires these same essentials?

Feeds me with the Living Bread

In our daily walk with God, we need the daily nourishment and refreshment from his Word. 'Your word is a lamp to my feet and a light to my path' (Psalm 119:105). 'If anyone thirsts, let him come to me and drink' (John 7:37).

Bible reading

Psalm 107:1–22

Prayer

Lord Jesus, I need you to be my companion and guide each day. May I come to you daily for your refreshment. May I hear you speak as I feed on your Word. Amen.

29. In everything give thanks

Now thank we all our God,
With hearts, and hands, and voices;
Who wondrous things hath done,
In whom his world rejoices;
Who, from our mothers' arms,
Hath blessed us on our way
With countless gifts of love,
And still is ours today.

No one knows better than our Lord that if we, his children, were to see the world exactly as the media portray it, we could easily feel sad and disheartened. We could find much to complain about. Because he doesn't want us to view our personal lives in a negative way, he encourages us to look for the good in everything, always! 'In everything give thanks; for this is the will of God in Christ Jesus for you' (1 Thessalonians 5:18).

Thankful hearts
It can help us so much if, when watching the news, we begin to 'count our blessings', mentally listing all the things in our lives we can give thanks for. The Lord knows that if we have a thankful heart instead of a complaining, ungrateful one, we will feel blessed, and our hearts will be filled with joy and peace, as he promised.

Thankful hands
There comes a time when we think the vacuum cleaner seems to have grown heavier; when the shops seem to have moved further away; the kitchen cupboards seem to be higher than they were! This is the time to accept that we can't always accomplish easily what we once did. What we can do is thank the Lord for what we are still able to do for ourselves and, hopefully, also for others.

Thankful voices
Thankfulness makes it easy and natural to bring the Lord into everyday

conversations. A friend greets us: 'Hello there, I haven't seen you for ages!' 'Oh yes, I can still do my own shopping. I thank the Lord every morning for all that I am able to do.' If we look out for opportunities to voice our thankfulness, we can find many, and it actually does make us feel better! A choirmaster once said to the congregation, 'Sing from your heart, and remember, God loves the crows as well as the nightingales!' We sing best when we sing from thankful hearts, hearts that are grateful to God for all his provision, and most of all, for our salvation.

Bible reading
Psalm 100

Prayer
Lord, I come with grateful thanks for the love that you have shown to me, and for the strength you give me day by day. I thank you that you provide for me in every way. Help me to begin each new day with a thankful heart, most of all for my Saviour, the Lord Jesus Christ. Amen.

30. A fairer land?

There's a land that is fairer than day,
And by faith we can see it afar:
For the Father waits over the way,
To prepare us a dwelling-place there.

Greener grass?
Here in the UK the weather is a favourite topic of conversation, maybe because it's so changeable. Often we hear people complaining, 'It's too wet/too cold/too hot!' Some decide to move abroad, longing for a less stressful lifestyle, to get away from business, traffic, politics, etc. They want to give their children a simple, healthier life, raising chickens, ducks and geese, growing vegetables, enjoying leisurely outdoor meals. We enjoy the TV programmes showing families making a new start. We follow the story as they buy a new home, learn the language, start new jobs, and we hope they make a success of it. Some brave senior citizens decide to retire to a warmer climate. We wonder whether it will all turn out to be as perfect as they dreamed it would be. Will they live to be 'happy ever after'?

The garden of Eden
I wonder whether longing for a perfect life is something deep within all of us, a feeling that this world, as it is, is not where we should be, a feeling that longs for what Adam and Eve once had and lost for all mankind through the Fall? It's as though we feel that this is not where we should be, or where we are fully content to be.

Perfect provision
God's first intention for mankind was a perfect climate, with perfect surroundings, occupations, peace, and love (Genesis 1–2). God would 'walk and talk with Adam' in the garden. Just imagine that: a perfect relationship with God! It was lost for us all because of disobedience. In return for their life in that perfect place (where they could have been perfectly satisfied for ever), Adam and Eve ignored God's only command. God knew the consequences of disobedience (Genesis 2:17). However, he is

the God of 'second chances', always loving, always ready to forgive, always with the solution of a Saviour, the Lord Jesus Christ. Adam and Eve suffered the consequences of their sin, but Jesus paid the price for it. Was our perfect home lost to us for ever? No! We read of the future: 'Now I saw a new heaven and a new earth, for the first heaven and the first earth had passed away ... Behold, the tabernacle of God is with men, and he will dwell with them, and they shall be his people' (Revelation 21:1,3).

Bible reading
Genesis 2

Prayer
Loving Father, thank you that the perfect place we long for, although not here, is waiting for us, if we are trusting our Saviour. Amen.

31. Peace, God's glorious river

Like a river, glorious,
Is God's perfect peace,
Over all victorious
In its bright increase;
Perfect, yet it floweth
Fuller ev'ry day—
Perfect, yet it groweth
Deeper all the way.

Hidden in the hollow
Of his blessèd hand,
Never foe can follow,
Never traitor stand;
Not a surge of worry,
Not a shade of care,
Not a blast of hurry
Touch the spirit there.

Quiet!

People long for peace. Mums cry out for it: 'Hush, let's have some peace and quiet in here!' Grandparents, one eye on the clock, wait for it when it's almost time for the children to return home after a visit. Wives, mothers, and families pray for it, as loved ones in the armed forces leave for war zones. People with troublesome neighbours are desperate for peace. But as we go about our normal daily lives, it seems that there is no peace. Reading some hymns, we know what the writer is saying, but sometimes we have to say, 'This person has found something I haven't yet learnt; how do I find peace?' The Bible tells us, 'You will keep him in prefect peace, whose mind is stayed on you, because he trusts in you. Trust in the LORD for ever, for in YAH, the LORD, is everlasting strength' (Isaiah 26:3–4). Paul teaches the Philippians:

…in everything by prayer and supplication, with thanksgiving, let your requests be made known to God; and the peace of God, which surpasses all understanding, will guard your hearts and minds through Christ Jesus. Finally, brethren, whatever things are true, whatever things are noble, … are just, … are pure, … are lovely, … are of good report, if there is any virtue, and … anything praiseworthy—meditate on these things. The things which you learned and received, heard and saw in me, these do, and the God of peace will be with you (4:6–9).

Well, that's quite a tall order and plenty for us to think about! We could think about the opposite of these things, but that would never bring peace to our minds.

Flowing every day
So how do we 'bring' this river of peace to our lives each day? We must begin our day with prayer, knowing from experience that 'life happens', no matter what our planned programme! We have to begin with our morning prayers, drawing deeply from the source of the 'glorious river', God's peace. Then we must keep close, returning to him throughout the day, no matter how busy we are. For he has promised to keep us at peace if we keep our thoughts towards him.

Bible reading
Psalm 119:156–176

Prayer
Father, without you this would be an impossible task. Help me to make a start learning the truth of this today. You have promised that your peace will grow deeper and fuller. Amen.

32. What a wonderful world!

My God, I thank thee, who hast made
The earth so bright,
So full of splendour and of joy,
Beauty and light;
So many glorious things are here,
Noble and right.

Full of splendour

No wonder Louis Armstrong's song *What a wonderful world* was a hit! In spite of the complaints we hear about wars, the weather, global warming, etc., many still recognize that our earthly home is filled with wonder, and lavish provision from 'the living God who gives us richly all things to enjoy' (1 Timothy 6:17) and care for (Genesis 2:15,19,23). In creation, God has done everything possible to communicate something of his beautiful creative thoughts to his children. It 'speaks' of the Creator.

Beauty and light

He tells us creation 'speaks' and that we should be receptive enough to hear! 'Day unto day utters speech, and night unto night reveals knowledge' (Psalm 19:2).

What can we 'hear'?

Jesus once silenced the Pharisees, who were grumbling because his followers were shouting his praises, by saying, 'If they didn't praise me, the very stones would cry out!' (Luke 19:40).

So many glorious things

Imagine we can hear some of these 'glorious things' speaking. They might sound something like this:

So bright and full of joy

Enter Sun, Moon and Stars: 'We are the lights that separate day from night, serving as signs to mark seasons, days and years, and giving light and warmth to the earth. Surely the One who made us, and put us in our places, has perfect knowledge, plus creative power, and rules all things.'

Enter Rose: 'I am a lovely colour, giving pleasure to all. I have form and shape. As I open my petals to the sun, I release my perfume and face my Creator, who must be far more beautiful than I am.'

Enter Blackbird: 'Wow! I can fly! The plans that went into my design must be from a powerful and sensitive God. He gave me a voice to sing his praises, and so he must like music too!'

Enter Music: 'Of course he does; he made the notes for man to manipulate into melodies. Like mathematics, music has laws.'

Enter Rainbow: 'Colours also have laws, and from my vantage point, I can tell you that perfumes and flavours do, also! Many great laws of physics and science are all too much for the tiny mind of man to take in. Our Creator is awesome!'

We won't let the animals speak—they would have so much to say, we wouldn't be able to get a word in edgeways!

Bible reading
Psalm 148

Prayer
Father God, thank you for your provision of so many beautiful things, all made for your pleasure, and for ours. Amen.

33. Exceedingly abundant love

Come, let us sing of a wonderful love,
Tender and true;
Out of the heart of the Father above,
Streaming to me and to you.
Wonderful love,
Dwells in the heart of the Father above.

'Pressed down and running over'

Once, your chin could hardly reach to the counter on the ice cream van. Do you remember waiting to hear the ice cream man ring the bell? Nothing electronic then, it was the same as the bell the teacher rang in the school yard.

We had two ice cream men. The first would reach down into the tub, and place the exact amount, one perfectly round scoop, balanced on top of the cornet! His face was very serious; I don't think he enjoyed his job! We were afraid to walk away with the ice cream in case the scoop fell off! The second man was different; he would get a scoop, press it down inside the cornet, then place another on top, and press that down until it overflowed the sides. We had to lick it before it melted. This is what is known as a 'generous' helping. God always gives in that way—'generously'.

Abundant giving

Modern Bible translations use an assortment of words to show the meaning of 'abundant': rich, generous, intense, immeasurable, increasing, plentiful, extensive, exceeding. These words help us to understand the way in which our heavenly Father gives, and desires to give, to us. The word abundant, or abundantly, is mentioned alongside the following gifts from our Father: pardon, grace, love, provision, and answered prayer. We wanted to give to our children, and we still want to give to our grandchildren. God wants to give to us. It's never done grudgingly, but always gladly, and always when we don't deserve it. When Moses threw down and broke the tablets of stone in anger, God treated him so graciously, by writing some more! Then he went on to explain something of his nature to Moses: '… The Lord God, merciful and gracious, longsuffering, and abounding in goodness and truth' (Exodus 34:6). This is just one small glimpse of the bountiful goodness of God the Father. The Son is the same as the Father, and works in just the same way (John 5:36).

Abundant life!

How grateful we are for the abundant love shown by the Father and the Son at the cross. How thankful we are for our Saviour's words, '… I have come that they may have life, and that they may have it more abundantly' (John 10:10).

Bible reading

Isaiah 55

Prayer

Father, thank you for your exceedingly abundant love that bought for us an abundant life now, and an abundant future ahead, through our Lord Jesus Christ. Amen.

34. God's 'tracking'

In heavenly love abiding, no change my heart shall fear;
And safe is such confiding, for nothing changes here:
The storm may roar without me, my heart may low be laid;
But God is round about me, and can I be dismayed?

Hazy, daisy, lazy days of summer

Children don't, or rather, can't, play outside in the way we were able to do. Sadly, it's no longer safe, so they will never experience that freedom we enjoyed. Those who lived out of town really roamed free! On leaving home in the morning, they would collect their friends along the way, and plan the next 'adventure'. Each one had a picnic of jam sandwiches and lemonade (warm before long!), and often didn't return home until 'tea-time'!

Tracking

Tracking was a favourite game we used to play. There were 'hiders' and 'chasers'. The hiders were given a count of one hundred, and running off, they left 'tracking signs' along the way. These were marks made on the stones with chalk, twigs or pebbles placed in an arrow shape, or long grasses tied in a knot, clues left along the path taken.

Where is God?

In the story of Job, because of all his terrible experiences—his loss of family, home, business, and finally health—he questioned where a loving God was in all this; when we read his story, who could blame him? His friends were no help; in fact, they made him feel worse. Some said he must have sinned badly to deserve all this 'bad luck'. They all had an opinion, but none was correct! Job tried to understand; he talked back to God, thinking God was his enemy: 'It's as if you have put marks on the soles of my feet so you can see each step I take in order to harm me!' (see Job 13:27).

God's constant 'tracking'

David had the right understanding, that God's 'tracking' was for his good. 'O LORD, you have searched me and known me. You know my sitting down and my rising up; You understand my thought afar off. You comprehend my path and my lying down, and are acquainted with all my ways' (Psalm 139:1–3). God's 'tracking' is always for our security, no matter how things appear. Maybe we don't understand now, but one day all will be made plain. 'But then I shall know just as I also am known' (1 Corinthians 13:12).

Bible readings
Job 1:6–12; 13:15; and 42:1–11

Prayer
Father, when troubles come to us, and we don't know the reason, help us to keep trusting, knowing that you are constantly with us in every struggle and difficulty. Give us strength to carry on, even when we don't understand, for, one day, 'I shall know just as I also am known.' Amen.

35. Run for cover

Things that once were wild alarms
Cannot now disturb my rest;
Closed in everlasting arms,
Pillowed on the loving breast:
Oh, to lie for ever here!
Doubt and care and self resign,
While he whispers in my ear—
I am his, and he is mine.

Where do we run for cover?

How often do you think about God during the day? Think over the words used in the Bible to give us a picture of his love, his desire to shelter and provide a covering of protection for us. He wants to commune with us all through the day, whatever we may be doing. Some people like to keep God in a special 'holy box' in their mind: to bring him out when they go to church, when they say their prayers, or read the Bible, then put him safely back again. Perhaps they haven't fully understood the Father–child relationship he so desires to have with us. He wants to be an integral part of our everyday lives. He has physically walked in our world; he is no stranger to it. Although he is holy, by his Spirit he dwells within us, and he fills the world with his presence. Start to watch and listen for his messages of love in the everyday things of life.

A shelter in the storm

'… For my soul trusts in you; and in the shadow of your wings I will make my refuge, until these calamities have passed by' (Psalm 57:1). 'How precious is your lovingkindness, O God! Therefore the children of men put their trust under the shadow of your wings' (Psalm 36:7).

Once, as I walked through the park by the playground, I was thinking about these verses. Suddenly, there was a very heavy downpour of rain. All the children scattered; three of the very youngest ones ran as fast as they could, but had to wait for the smallest one, who started to cry. Across the field, their father ran quickly towards them. He was holding up a brightly coloured golf umbrella. By the time he reached them, they were soaking wet. They flung themselves at him, as he put one arm around their shoulders and drew them close to him, comforting them. The tears soon stopped! 'Thank you, Lord,' I said as I hurried on. 'I couldn't have a better picture than that!'

Bible reading
Psalm 63

Prayer
Father, when I receive bad news; when I feel lonely and vulnerable; in all circumstances that could make me anxious, may you draw me close, to shelter me in your arms of love, where you have promised to keep and protect me. Amen.

36. From start to finish

Run the straight race through God's good grace,
Lift up thine eyes, and seek his Face;
Life with its way before thee lies,
Christ is the path, and Christ thy prize.

There is great excitement each time the Olympic Games come around. Weeks before, sports commentators start discussing every aspect. This is especially the case when they are held in our country. The spectacular opening ceremony unfolds and we watch the world's best sportsmen and women proudly enter the stadium, wearing their smart blazers and representing their country. Every face is smiling with expectation. The cheering crowds encourage them. Even those who have no sporting interests can enjoy the spectacle. We are all united as together we watch the lone runner enter, effortlessly mount the steps, and light the Olympic Torch. The participants are aware of their supporters urging them forward as they look towards the finishing tape.

Run the straight race

It's quite likely that the apostle Paul witnessed a race himself, for the Games originated in Greece. He compares the Christian journey to a race we all have to 'run'. Often, when tired and weary, we wonder why we have to experience life's troubles, yet constantly we find that, when we ask Jesus, he gives us more faith.

Lift up thine eyes

We think of the amount of exercise and practice required by runners, reminding us that our faith grows stronger with practice too. God is always working out his purpose for us, to fulfil his desire that we stay 'on track' and eventually spend eternity with him. Dependency brings us closer to him than independence!

Christ thy prize

We must continually look to Jesus, who has promised to keep us and to finish what he started when we first believed, until the 'finishing tape'. His eternal life is our reward. Always remember Jesus' words that he will finish in us what he began when he first brought us to faith.

Bible reading
Hebrews 11–12:3

Prayer
Lord Jesus, when we first began our Christian life we were full of enthusiasm; faith wasn't difficult, and you made special allowances for us. Just as we supported our children when they were learning to walk, so you often led us on easy pathways. We have been 'on the way' many years now, and have experienced sorrow, heartache, pain, and bereavement. We are sad when we remember the times when it was so difficult that we almost gave up, but you promised to lift us up each time we asked, and you did just that, setting us on our feet once again! Thank you, Lord. If there are any today who did fall, or any that have never begun, we know that you are waiting for them just to look to you, and that the faith they need is always available. Amen.

37. I'll be loving you always

All scenes alike engaging prove
To souls impressed with sacred love;
Where'er they dwell, they dwell in thee,
In heav'n, in earth, or on the sea.
While place we seek, or place we shun,
The soul finds happiness in none;
But with my God to guide my way,
'Tis equal joy to go or stay.

Changes

People don't like change, do they? Many have seen their home towns change beyond recognition: whole streets bulldozed away, towns made so uniform we could be in any High Street in the land. What about the local supermarket? When they have a 'shelf shuffle' and the layout is changed, just listen to the grumbles! People can't follow their shopping lists in order anymore, and they don't like it! Those of us in the UK will remember when decimal currency was introduced. There was a joke that went round: 'They ought to wait until all the old people have died before it's changed!' Sadly, many seniors find it necessary to move house; what a big change that is!

Through all the changing scenes of life

How thankful we are to be told our God is unchangeable. He wants to comfort us with that thought, and tells us, 'For I am the LORD, I do not change' (Malachi 3:6). 'Every good gift and every perfect gift is from above, and comes down from the Father of lights, with whom there is no variation or shadow of turning' (James 1:17). While everything else around us is changing so fast, our God will never change through all eternity, and our Saviour, the Lord Jesus Christ, will remain the same for ever.

Childhood days

Do you remember your days in Sunday school, your teacher, singing choruses? There is still comfort recalling words over again.

It is a thing most wonderful,
Almost too wonderful to be,
That God's own Son should come from heaven
And die to save a child like me.

Those thoughts haven't changed. Do you remember 'giving your heart to Jesus', asking him 'to be your Saviour'? If you did that, what a comfort it is to know that his promise of love and forgiveness still stands. Even after many years, his promises don't change. But if you didn't ask him then, you can still ask him now. He is always true to his name 'Saviour', the one 'unchanging' person.

Bible reading
Psalm 90

Prayer
Lord Jesus, I thank you, as I think back to that 'happy day' I received you as my Saviour. It's wonderful to know that you have kept me throughout my life, and will continue to do so. I come to you again now for forgiveness and restoration, and I trust you, Lord, for the rest of my days. Amen.

38. Who do you think you are?

Breathe on me, Breath of God,
Fill me with life anew,
That I may love what thou dost love,
And do what thou wouldst do.

Breathe on me, Breath of God,
Till I am wholly thine.
Till all this earthly part of me
Glows with thy fire divine.

Who am I?

For many of us, any relatives before our great-great-grandparents remain a mystery. It seems to be a popular and interesting pastime nowadays, to discover your family tree. As Christians, before we do that, first of all it is good to be sure of our heritage from God, for it is only in him that we find our true 'worth'. It is interesting to watch on TV as celebrities laugh and cry on discovering their various background histories. They find many surprises. It seems that some find it to be a humbling experience.

Have you ever wondered just who *you* are? The Bible has wonderful verses telling us, sometimes in brief sentences, astonishing truths about that; these can astound us if we really think about what God's words are saying. Once we have taken in this information and found our true worth, we can love ourselves as God expects us to, and so love others also (Leviticus 19:18)!

The breath of God

'… And the LORD God formed man of the dust of the ground, and breathed into his nostrils the breath of life; and man became a living being' (Genesis 2:7).

Royal descent

'But *you* are a chosen generation, a royal priesthood, a holy nation, his own special people ...' (1 Peter 2:9). Most of us have heard or read about how and where our 'family tree' began. Through a careful reading of Genesis 1–2, looking especially where 'man' is mentioned, we meet with a loving, creator God, who didn't have to make mankind: he wanted to (Genesis 1:26)! His heart of love was behind every thought and action towards mankind. He provided everything for his provision: comfort, blessing and position (Genesis 1:7–15,18). Also he gave just one command for man's own protection (Genesis 2:16–17)! In Genesis 3 we see original sin and its consequences!

Breathe on me, Breath of God,
Until my heart is pure,
Until with thee I will one will,
To do and to endure.

Bible reading
Romans 8

Prayer
Father God, I thank you that, because of your Son, I am adopted into your family [Galatians 4:1–7]. I gratefully take my place and accept my rich heritage, remembering always that I am made in your image [Genesis 1:27]. Sometimes, I find that hard to believe, because I know I am a sinner. Thank you, Father, for Jesus, who lives always to pray for me [Hebrews 7:25]. Please make me 'wholly thine'. Thank you, Father. Amen.

39. A time for everything

Today thy mercy calls me, to wash away my sin;
However great my trespass, whate'er I may have been.
However long from mercy I may have turned away,
Thy blood, O Christ, can cleanse me, and make me white today.

Time past

'To everything there is a season, a time for every purpose' (Ecclesiastes 3:1–8).

Time flies! Can you remember the clock from your childhood home, or the school clock? Its fingers moved so slowly then! Do you remember the town clock, where people met? The station clock, where they parted? Not forgetting the hated alarm clock on cold winter mornings! God was calling you even back then! Wise King Solomon spoke of some appointed times, notably 'a time for birth and death' (Ecclesiastes 3:2).

No doubt we could add more life experiences to Solomon's list—a time to marry, and a time to lose a partner; to have children, and then to let them go; to have grandchildren; to go into hospital and to recover; lonely anniversaries and family celebrations. Some memories can bring smiles of satisfaction; others, regrets. There are things we would like to change but can't. Whatever can we do, when we realize time has passed us by, leaving many events unresolved and unforgiven?

Time present—today's the day!

God our eternal Father is still calling. 'Behold, now is the accepted time; now is the day of salvation' (2 Corinthians 6:2). Never think it's too late to answer. 'Trust in him at all times, you people; pour out your heart before him; God is a refuge for us' (Psalm 62:8). The hymn continues to speak to us. Sometimes, it's helpful thoughtfully to recite the words:

O, all-embracing mercy, thou ever open door,
What should I do without thee, when heart and eyes run o'er?
When all things seem against us, to drive us to despair,
We know one gate is open, one ear will hear our prayer.

Today thy gate is open, and all who enter in,
Shall find a Father's welcome, and pardon for their sin;
The past shall be forgotten, a present joy be given,
A future grace be promised—a glorious crown in heaven.

Bible reading
Psalm 103

Time future—Prayer
Father, my life has passed so quickly. Please assure me of the grace and help you offer right now, bringing your peace to my thoughts, enabling me to look forward to that wonderful future in heaven awaiting those whose sins have been forgiven. This is so much better than regretting things from the past that I cannot change. Please forgive, and receive me now, in the Name of the Lord Jesus Christ. Amen.

40. Count your blessings

Count your blessings, name them one by one,
Count your blessings, see what God hath done;
Count your blessings, name them one by one,
And it will surprise you what the Lord hath done.

One to one

Sometimes when we visit the sick or lonely, it seems like a wasted afternoon. When it's time to leave, we don't feel our words, prayers or gifts have helped them, and they certainly haven't made it easy for us. At the same time, how very often the folk with the most to complain about don't seem to complain much at all! In fact, when we leave, we find the visit has been of mutual benefit. The fellowship, prayers and laughter shared has been worthwhile—we are both blessed from time spent together. These kinds of people are never short of visitors!

One by one

Kay is a lady who always 'counts her blessings'! She has just celebrated her ninetieth birthday, surrounded by family and friends. She lives in a small bungalow, with a warden on call, who 'pops in' to make sure she is all right each morning. She usually is unless, between yesterday's teatime and today's breakfast, she has had another 'good idea' or plan, requiring someone else to make it a reality! Gradually losing the ability to do many of the things she once enjoyed, she replaced them with 'all things bright and beautiful'. She lives quite happily now, surrounded by lots of furniture (to 'hold on to when I wobble!'). Although her bungalow is filled with mementos, flowers, plants and photographs, she can always find a little space for something else! Many of the photos of relatives are sepia, the subjects just a memory. Some are digital proofs of her many new friends (she tends to collect more as time goes by!). 'You can choose your friends; you can't choose your relatives,' she says.

Name them one by one

She values friends, with Jesus at the top of her list! She expresses her thanks to God continually for him, plus the following list—family and friends, dog and cat, garden and birds, classical music, books, colours, flowers, stars and rainbows.

Heaven above is softer blue,
Earth around is sweeter green;
Something lives in every hue
Christless eyes have never seen:
Birds with gladder songs o'erflow,
Flowers with deeper beauties shine,
Since I know, as now I know,
I am his and he is mine.

Kay knows!

Bible reading
Ecclesiastes 5:10–20

Prayer
Father, when I go to visit someone, or if I am visited, please be present with us, and may I always remember that you are my permanent 'house guest'. Thank you. Amen.

41. With Christ is far better

Jesus, thou art all compassion,
Pure, unbounded love thou art;
Visit us with thy salvation,
Enter every trembling heart.

Immediately with Christ

A dear friend of mine watched as, in spite of many prayers, the doctors turned off her daughter's life support machine. The seventeen-year-old breathed her last and immediately was in the presence of her Saviour. She was a committed Christian!

There had been no warning signs. Forty-eight hours previously, my son and I were standing beside her at a gospel service, all happily singing, 'Bringing in the sheaves'. At the time of the funeral, my husband was not a Christian, but we attended it together. At the request of the family, the gospel message was included; our pastor led us through the service with sensitive, beautiful words, comforting to family and Christians alike, then gave a clear gospel message of the love of Jesus and his desire that we should all trust him completely 'while we still had the opportunity'. My husband, for the first time, accepted the gospel invitation! Today, he is in that perfect place where Christ awaits us. Martyn Lloyd-Jones wrote the following words:

Matthew Henry explained, 'We are never told in the Scriptures that we should look forward to death; but we are told very frequently that we should look forward to heaven.' The man who looks forward to death simply wants to get out of life because of his troubles. That is not Christian … The Christian has a positive desire for heaven … But, more than this, what do we look forward to? … Is it the freedom from sin? Is it the rest of heaven? Is it the peace of heaven? Is it the joy of heaven? All these things are to be found there, thank God; but that is not the thing to look forward to in heaven. It is the face of God … Do we long for that? Paul tells us to die is 'to be with Christ.' There is no need to add anything to that. That is why, I believe, we are told so little in the detailed sense about the life in heaven and the glory. I will tell you what heaven is. It is 'to be with Christ' and if that does not satisfy you, then you do not know Christ at all …'[1]

On young Rebecca's memorial stone it says, 'With Christ which is much better.'

Bible reading
Revelation 21

Prayer
Finish then thy new creation,
Pure and spotless may we be;
Let us see thy whole salvation
Perfectly secured by thee!
Changed from glory into glory,
Till in heaven we take our place;
Till we cast our crowns before thee,
Lost in wonder, love and praise.

Note

1. **D. Martyn Lloyd-Jones,** *Faith on Trial: Studies in The Sermon on the Mount* (London: Inter-Varsity Press, 1973), p. 111.

42. Come unto me and rest

I heard the voice of Jesus say,
'Come unto me and rest:
Lay down, thou weary one, lay down
Thy head upon my breast.'

I came to Jesus as I was—
Weary, and worn, and sad;
I found in him a resting place,
And he has made me glad.

How many roles have you fulfilled during your life? To see them listed may surprise you: father, mother, son, daughter, brother, sister, pupil, teacher, husband, wife, aunt, uncle, cousin, friend, neighbour, church member, carer… We have all had some of these, and maybe many more roles. Looking back in a positive way, it can be encouraging to think of what has been accomplished. However, can we truthfully say that every period of our life has been totally enjoyable?

Come unto me and rest

Over the years, how many times have we turned to Jesus for help when we felt the pressures all too much to bear alone? Did we take advantage of his invitation to 'rest in him'? For he knew well what it meant to be tired and weary. The popular *Footsteps* poem speaks of us being 'carried' during times of trouble, and Jesus is the one who carries us. His offer still stands: 'Come to me, all you who labour and are heavy laden, and I will give you rest' (Matthew 11:28). Do we believe that, and trust him?

Returning and resting with confidence

We have the Father's reassurance that 'in returning and rest you shall be saved; In quietness and confidence shall be your strength' (Isaiah 30:15). 'Even to your old age, I am he, and even to grey hairs I will carry you!' (Isaiah 46:4). Maybe you are not returning, but coming to him for the first time. Forgiveness and grace are available for you. Loving arms are just waiting to carry you through, for the rest of your life.

Bible reading
Psalm 121

Prayer
Lord Jesus, I need you all the time, not just in times of trouble. Please help me to accept from you all that you have promised to those who need you as Saviour. Amen.

43. Face to face

Face to face with Christ my Saviour,
Face to face—what will it be?
When with rapture I behold him,
Jesus Christ who died for me.

> Face to face shall I behold him,
> Far beyond the starry sky;
> Face to face in all his glory,
> I shall see him by and by!

Only faintly now I see him,
With the darkling veil between,
But a blessèd day is coming,
When his glory shall be seen.

Face to face! O blissful moment!
Face to face—to see and know!
Face to face with my Redeemer,
Jesus Christ who loves me so.

Far beyond the starry sky

If you took your grandchildren to see the film *Toy Story*, perhaps you
remember the spaceman Buzz Lightyear shouting 'To infinity and beyond!'
as he attempted to launch into outer space. I wonder whether he realized
just what he was saying? For infinity, like God, has no boundaries. Perhaps
it's just as well Buzz wasn't successful! The first astronauts on the moon
weren't surprised they didn't find heaven or God sitting on a throne
somewhere out there! Instead, when viewing our tiny but beautiful earth
from that vantage point, and overwhelmed at the sight, one of them simply
quoted, 'In the beginning, God created the heavens and the earth' (Genesis
1:1). The Bible tells us that heaven is a very real place in a real location.

Then and now

'For now we see in a mirror, dimly, but then face to face. Now I know in part, but then I shall know just as I also am known' (1 Corinthians 13:12). All questions and things we don't understand here will be answered in heaven one day! Jesus has gone there before us and waits for all who have trusted him now to enter into his glorious presence then! He tells us something of what he will be doing in the meantime: he will be praying for us continually.

In my Father's house are many mansions; if it were not so, I would have told you. I go to prepare a place for you ... I will come again and receive you to myself; that where I am, there you may be also. And where I go you know, and the way you know ... I am the way, the truth, and the life. No one comes to the Father except through me' (John 14:2–6).

Before he ascended to his father, Jesus said, 'Thomas, because you have seen me, you have believed. Blessed are those who have not seen and yet have believed' (John 20:29). What encouragement for us!

Bible reading
John 17

Prayer
Thank you, Lord, because now I place my faith in you alone, I shall be with you in heaven one day, for all eternity. Amen.

44. Faith's resting place

My faith has found a resting place,
Not in device nor creed;
I trust the ever-living One,
His wounds for me shall plead.
I need no other argument, I need no other plea,
It is enough that Jesus died, and that he died for me.

Have you ever told a mountain to 'Clear off into the sea'? I haven't, and don't know anyone who has, although I have known many answers to prayer in what seemed to be impossible situations! However, if Jesus said we could move mountains, then we can! The provision of faith is there—we just need more!

Faith resting

Where would we be without our faith in Jesus, our own 'resting place'? Christian faith begins with the faith God gives, and by that faith, plus his grace, we will continue in it to the end, 'finishing well', '… by faith in the Son of God who loved me and gave himself for me' (Galatians 2:20). What a wonderful relationship! We, totally trusting, and Jesus, continuing to strengthen our faith more each time we use it.

Faith v. devices

Satan hates saving faith—he is a liar with evil devices! He will use every opportunity to try to rob us, and our children and grandchildren, of faith, as evolutionary theories are taught, without considering a Creator! He is waiting, at schools, universities, and TV studios, to focus the spotlight on questions, discussion and argument, so diverting it from the cross of Christ where it belongs. Pray for young people, that although they may have questions, their faith in the Lord Jesus will stand firm. Satan can create nothing but chaos, misery and destruction. He knows his final destination, and is determined to take as many souls as possible with him.

It is enough that Jesus died ...

Will God's question on judgement day be, 'Did you believe in creation or evolution?' No! The question will be, 'Did you put your faith in my beloved Son?'

... And that he died for me

Is our faith tried and tested? Yes! Is it sometimes weak and wobbly? Yes! Does Jesus understand that? YES! Just before Jesus died, Peter's faith was weak. Jesus knows our frailties, just as he knew Peter's beforehand, and told him, 'But I have prayed for you, that your faith should not fail'(Luke 22:31–32). Jesus expects us to believe that we can totally trust him, for he continually prays for our faith.

Bible readings

Hebrews 11:1–40; 12:1–3

Prayer

Father, thank you for my faith in Jesus. Encourage me to place all my faith in you alone. In anxious times of doubt, may I draw closer to my 'resting place'. Amen.

45. The good old days

O God, our help in ages past,
Our hope for years to come,
Our shelter from the stormy blast,
And our eternal home.

I think we often view the past through rose-coloured glasses! Did it really never rain in the summertime?

Our help in ages past

Remember Washing Day? The steamy clothes drying around the fire? Washing really did take all day! How words can bring back memories: copper boiler; dolly tub; mangle; and faithful old clothes maiden. All usually the housewives' responsibilities. Not forgetting the men's chores, which included cleaning out the grate, taking out the ashes, and bringing in the coal—nutty slack to 'keep the home fires burning'! Maybe those memories bring a smile with them!

But maybe it wasn't so rosy after all! Did we ever give God a thought in those days? Did we realize that God was caring for us, and calling us to himself right back then? 'Remember now your Creator in the days of your youth, before the difficult days come, and the years draw near when you say, "I have no pleasure in them"' (Ecclesiastes 12:1).

Our hope for years to come

In his great patience and love, God never gives up on us; it's as though he just waits quietly 'in the wings'. What condescension! Still, many go on through decades without him. Well, perhaps they have said a quick prayer in an emergency! Were they too busy to hear? Did they think they could manage this life *alone*? Maybe some stopped going to church through a bad experience there. 'I didn't like the minister', or 'No one spoke to me'; 'I sat in a pew and someone asked me to move, as, they explained, it was their seat'! Many people dismiss God from their lives because of some incident that happened years ago. Now these excuses sound a bit lame—they're not God's fault, surely? He still loves, and still waits.

A thousand ages in thy sight are like an evening—GONE!

'The harvest is past, the summer is ended, and we are not saved!' (Jeremiah 8:20). These words sound so sad and so hopeless, don't they? They need never be spoken by us. The same God that called in our youth still calls us today. He tells us, 'I have loved you with an everlasting love' (Jeremiah 31:3). Please don't let something long passed spoil your chance of present, and future, happiness.

Bible reading

John 6:32–40

Prayer

Father God, thank you for your love and patience towards me. Forgive me for living through dangerous times unaware of your care. Please accept me today, through Jesus Christ. Amen.

46. Just for you

There's a work for Jesus ready at your hand,
'Tis a task the Master just for you has planned.
Haste to do his bidding, yield him service true;
There's a work for Jesus none but you can do.

Chelsea Pensioners

Have you ever watched the 'boys of the old brigade' in the Remembrance Day Service? How proudly they march down the steps and across the Royal Albert Hall, to great acclaim, wearing their shining medals, reminding us of their gallant service for king and country! One day we all hope to hear our Lord say to us, 'Well done, thou good and faithful servant.'

What's your job?

Many major companies realize at last that senior citizens have much to offer, and are now employing them. For some of us, full-time work would be too much; we can't continue morning, noon and night without resting in-between, and we often find our minds making appointments our bodies can't keep! Even so, the Bible seems to encourage us actively to continue in the Lord's work. If he calls us to a task, he will equip us for it. He will never place unrealistic demands upon us, nor demand work beyond our capabilities, and we only have to ask for his grace and daily strength to help us. The needs are all around us.

A young spring chicken!

A promise from the Psalms still speaks to us: 'Those who are planted in the house of the LORD shall flourish in the courts of our God. They shall still bear fruit in old age; they shall be fresh and flourishing to declare that the LORD is upright ...' (Psalm 92:13–15). God also gave this lovely promise to Israel, when they were nearing the Promised Land: '... as your days, so shall your strength be' (Deuteronomy 33:25). Therefore, we must show ourselves willing, and he will provide the grace and strength. We can say confidently, 'I will go in the strength of the Lord GOD; I will make mention of your righteousness, of yours only. O God, you have taught me from my youth; ...

Now also when I am old and greyheaded, O God, do not forsake me, until I declare your strength to this generation ... (Psalm 71:16–18).

Only you can do it!

Do you know anyone to tell the gospel to? Perhaps a relative, neighbour, or friend, who has never heard of the love and forgiveness offered in our Lord Jesus Christ? Maybe that's the work that only you can do!

Bible reading

Psalm 71

Prayer

Dear Lord Jesus, grant me opportunities, through your Holy Spirit, to speak of your salvation to those around me. Help me to see them as lost, until you find them and they find you. Amen.

47. Marching on

Marching on in the light of God,
Marching on, I'm marching on:
Up the path that the Master trod,
Marching, marching on.

A robe of white, a crown of gold,
A harp, a home, a mansion fair,
A victor's palm, a joy untold,
Are mine when I get there.

Marching on through the hosts of sin,
Marching on, I'm marching on:
Victory's mine while I've Christ within,
Marching, marching on.

Marching on

Yes, there are many 'Christian soldiers' still 'marching on', even if it is a little slower these days! The country and western song says, 'This world is not my home, I'm just a passin' through.' I think we become more aware of that as the years go by. The Bible describes our life here on earth as a temporary thing, and Christians as sojourners, pilgrims, aliens and strangers in the world. Do you travel in this way, keeping your promised destination in view? We should do. We should be always confidently looking forward. Age brings no special privileges (well, maybe the bus pass!), and on the way from earth to heaven we never become immune to temptations. The Christian life is always a battle. The devil still thinks there is a possibility of causing us to 'give up' fighting the good fight. However, we have God's precious promises, and we are encouraged to press on '…looking unto Jesus, the author and finisher of our faith …' (Hebrews 12:2). We should be calling on the Name of the Lord Jesus at all times. This is a powerful Name, and anyone can call, in any situation. 'Resist the devil and he will flee from you' (James 4:7). At Calvary, Jesus fought and won the battle for us, so we are already victorious—the devil just hasn't understood this yet! So keep your eye on your reward! Many seniors are fit and well, but even if we are in that group, we are still aware of the many walking sticks, Zimmers, shopping walkers and motorized scooters there are these days.

Christ within

Reading through the hymn, some may smile at the 'marching' bit and may be thinking, 'For me, it's more like, "limping on"'! More and more we find ourselves turning to the Lord for every need, recognizing the truth of his words, as we discover: 'In quietness and confidence shall be your strength' (Isaiah 30:15).

Bible reading

Hebrews 11:1–16

Prayer

Lord, I know that you too have felt tired and weary; you know, more than anyone, all about pain. When I find life to be a struggle, help me to lean on your 'everlasting arms'; keep me 'marching on' in faith, in your strength, in your Name. Amen.

48. I've started, so I'll finish

I will sing the wondrous story
Of the Christ who died for me;
How he left his home in glory,
For the cross on Calvary.
Yes, I'll sing the wondrous story
Of the Christ who died for me;
Sing it with the saints in glory,
Gathered by the crystal sea.

I was lost; but Jesus found me—
Found the sheep that went astray;
Threw his loving arms around me,
Drew me back into his way …
He will keep me till the river
Rolls its waters at my feet;
Then he'll bear me safely over,
Where the loved ones I shall meet.

Many things are started and never finished: DIY; handicrafts; hobbies. What happens to that first flush of enthusiasm, I wonder? I could tell you about an embroidered tablecloth, begun the year of my engagement and not finished for my ruby wedding!

A 'wondrous story'

At my conversion (by then I was a wife and mother), I was thrilled to hear the simplicity of the gospel message: 'Believe on the Lord Jesus Christ and you will be saved …' (Acts 16:31); 'Behold, I stand at the door and knock. If anyone hears my voice and opens the door, I will come in to him and dine with him, and he with me' (Revelation 3:20). I thankfully replied, 'Lord, I didn't know you were there; I didn't realize you were interested in individual people. I always believed you were the Almighty God, but, as I read the Bible, I see you love us as your individual children, no matter what our age.'

The Christ who died for me

I continued to pray, 'You sent your beloved son to die for us, taking all our punishment for every sin. What a relief to know that, once I confess my sins and put my faith and trust in you, everlasting life is promised to me, and, when I die, there is a place in heaven reserved for me, all through my dear Saviour.' Yet I still remember thinking, 'I do hope I can keep this up!'

He will keep me

As I began to read the Bible, my doubts were soon dispelled. Wonderful verses assured me that to 'finish' wasn't up to me! I wouldn't be left alone to carry on! He would be with me, helping, all the way! '… Looking unto Jesus, the author and finisher of our faith … (Hebrews 12:2); '… being confident of this very thing, that he who has begun a good work in you will complete it until the day of Jesus Christ' (Philippians 1:6).

Bible reading

1 Corinthians 15:1–28

Prayer

Lord Jesus, when the day comes for me to cross that river, you will 'bear me safely over' into heaven, for ever. Thank you. Amen.

49. God's messengers

Angel voices, ever singing
Round thy throne of light,
Angel harps, for ever ringing,
Rest not day nor night;
Thousands only live to bless thee,
And confess thee Lord of might.

We mustn't believe everything we hear or read these days about angels! There are so many fanciful ideas that can mislead gullible followers. On Christmas cards, we are accustomed to seeing famous artists' impressions of angels, with their long golden curls, flowing white robes, and haloes! But angels have much more important work to do than simply to lie about on clouds playing harps all day! The Bible has a surprising amount of angel information, and what we read can amaze us.

'Angels from the realms of glory, wing their flight o'er all the earth'
The sheer number of angels is astounding: Hebrews 12:22 indicates that there are tens upon tens of thousands of them! As messengers of God, they can travel faster than the speed of light between heaven and earth, at God's command. Their work is on our behalf, for our good. They don't have physical bodies—they are spiritual beings—but they can take on a human 'appearance', at God's command, when given a task. We read in some accounts of where miraculous help is given by angels to individuals in certain desperate situations. This was written for our comfort: 'For he shall give his angels charge over you, to keep you in all your ways' (Psalm 91:11). Angels are described as bright and shining beings, emanating brilliant light, mirroring something of God's glory. Often, when angels appear visibly, people fall to the ground, overwhelmed by their radiance and power.

Despite the 6 o'clock news
The Bible indicates that angelic forces are ever fighting the continuous 'cosmic battle' against Satan and his evil. Although the times in which we

live are evil, the Bible has already warned us there will be 'wars and rumours of wars', yet, we are assured, God is still 'on the throne', and his angelic forces are in control of the battle, so we can have confidence. Satan is already defeated; he lost the battle when our Saviour died on the cross. That was where the victory was won *finally*! Satan has only a short time left; he is only loose for a little while. Because he knows his final destination, he is determined to take as many souls as possible. The day is coming when Jesus will return as he promised, to claim his victory and to proclaim his everlasting kingdom; to gather all believers to himself eternally.

Bible reading
Revelation 14

Prayer
Father God, surrounded in your glory by myriads of angels constantly praising you, thank you that we too can approach your throne, with our concerns, in the Name of our dear Saviour. Amen.

50. At the pearly gates

When I soar to realms of glory,
And an entrance I await,
If I whisper, 'Jesus only!'
Wide will ope the pearly gate;

When I join the heavenly chorus,
And the angel-hosts I see,
Precious Jesus, 'Jesus only',
Will my theme of rapture be.

Make sure you have your passport to heaven!

If you've been at the airport check-in when someone has forgotten his or her passport, or has found it to be out of date or unacceptable, you will have heard panic, anger, and frustration expressed! This is something that could be a picture of our arrival at the pearly gates one day! We expect those gates to swing open wide for us!

I can remember reading in an obituary column the following poem:

St Peter stood at the top of the stairs and softly whispered 'Come.'
The gates of heaven opened wide, and in walked Mum!

I had to smile as I visualized this little silver-haired old lady, carrying her supermarket shopping bag, walking eagerly forward into the glorious presence of God Almighty! Of course, this wouldn't happen. Perhaps if we were to imagine it was Peter who would be 'on the door' as people arrived, it would be much more like the following scene. Peter: 'What right have you to enter? What is the password?' You might answer, 'Well, my life has not been as bad as some people's, and better than many'; or 'I have done many good deeds, and been an excellent friend and neighbour, and never missed church'; or 'I always made the refreshments after the service, and I have sung in the choir for twenty years'; or even, 'I was an elder/deacon/steward/curate/minister.' But whatever reason we may think earns us a place in heaven, it can never be good enough.

Our passport is a gift from Jesus.
Receive it gladly and thankfully

God once spoke a message through the prophet Isaiah with words that could seem offensive to many, but which bring us to acknowledge that we could never, by trying our best, save ourselves: 'You are indeed angry, for we have sinned … and we need to be saved. But we are all like an unclean thing, and all our righteousnesses are like filthy rags' (Isaiah 64:5–6). Once we accept these words, this is our problem. But God has already provided the answer: 'Jesus Christ of Nazareth, whom you crucified… Nor is there salvation in any other, for there is no other name under heaven given among men by which we must be saved' (Acts 4:10–12). Here is our password into heaven: 'Jesus'. Jesus only! 'Nothing in my hand I bring, simply to thy cross I cling.'

Bible reading
2 Corinthians 5

Prayer
Lord Jesus, I have all eternity to discover even more about you. I can never thank you enough. My trust is all you require. Amen.

51. Eternal Light!

Eternal Light! Eternal Light! How pure the soul must be,
When, placed within thy searching sight,
It shrinks not, but, with calm delight,
Can live, and look on thee!

Anything to declare?

I wonder why we can sometimes feel just a little uncomfortable when we pass through Customs? There comes the time when we have to choose which queue to join: 'To declare' or 'Nothing to declare.' Having chosen, we can still have a vague, 'niggly' feeling, even when we know we have nothing to declare! When driving, our foot may move automatically to the brake pedal when we see a police car approaching or following us, even before we have checked our speed!

It's called 'Guilt'

Depending on our conscience, we can all experience the feeling of guilt, sometimes even falsely. If we know it's deserved, we need to confess it. However, with trust in our Saviour regarding our confessed sins, we can say with Paul, 'There is now *no* condemnation to those who are *in* Christ Jesus, who do not walk according to the flesh, but according to the Spirit' (Romans 8:1). Yes, 'He took all our guilt and shame, when he died and rose again'!

I wonder what thoughts go through your mind as you read the verse from *Eternal Light*? Some may just wonder what it means. Some of those words could really scare us, as we read about the holiness of God, and his hatred of sin. They could make us 'quake in our shoes' if we had never heard of the wondrous provision and love of our heavenly Father.

Our sin problem

Verse 3 of the hymn speaks of our problem.

Oh how shall I, whose native sphere is dark, whose mind is dim,
Before the Ineffable appear?

To us it seems an impossibility. Yet God will never just leave us in the dark with our guilt and fear. He is continually reaching out to us with the answer. First, he makes us face up to our problem, the guilt of our sin.

His costly solution

Then, he provides the solution, already prepared and agreed in love between the Father, Son, and Holy Spirit: on our behalf, Jesus was willingly sacrificed on the cross. Verse 5 says,

These, these prepare us for the sight of Holiness above:
The sons of ignorance and night
May dwell in the Eternal Light,
Through the Eternal Love!

Bible readings

Deuteronomy 33:18–23; Romans 5:1–21

Prayer

Dear loving, heavenly Father, thank you for sending the Lord Jesus to die in my place, to pay the price of my sins, to remove all punishment, guilt and shame, then to give me, one day, the joy of living in the presence of your 'Eternal Light'. Amen.

52. When the roll is called up yonder

When the trumpet of the Lord shall sound, and time shall be no more,
And the morning breaks, eternal, bright and fair;
When the saved of earth shall gather over on the other shore,
And the roll is called up yonder I'll be there.

Jesus is coming!
Old Testament prophets often wrote about the promised Saviour without understanding their words! We have the benefit of hindsight, and recognize their meaning. How blessed we are to read many prophecies about Jesus already fulfilled, giving us confidence that the few still unfulfilled will surely happen.

Prophecies fulfilled—Mary
The angel Gabriel brought some prophetic words from God to Mary about the future birth of her baby (Luke 1:26–38). He told her what to name the child and, more astounding, how this would happen, and just who her baby would be: 'the Son of God' (v. 35)! Can you imagine how shocked Mary must have felt? Her troubled thoughts? What a special young maid God had chosen to nurture his Son within her womb, in perfect submission to God the Holy Spirit. It wasn't long before she gave her response, in complete obedience. Read her reply (vv. 46–56). She was obviously familiar with prophecies!

Prophecies fulfilled—Joseph
What a gracious and obedient man God had chosen in Joseph, sending the 'angel of the Lord' (Matthew 1:18–25), who told him: '"Behold, the virgin shall be with child, and bear a Son, and they shall call his name Immanuel", which is translated "God with us"' (v. 23). He was repeating the words of Isaiah 7:14. 'You shall call his name JESUS, for he will save his people from their sins' (v. 21). Despite Joseph's disappointment and confusion, these

words stirred him to immediate obedience (v. 24). Whenever God has given a message for angels or prophets to foretell, it has always been accurate, and has always happened. Or will happen!

A prophecy waiting to happen—anytime!
Many Scriptures speak of the second coming of Jesus. Some, spoken by our loving Saviour, are not to make us afraid, but rather to warn us, 'for he is not willing that any should perish but that all should come to repentance' (2 Peter 3:9). When the roll is called, will you be there? Trust in him now, while there is still the opportunity. Matthew 24 contains a warning, only fearful to anyone who has not yet made sure of their salvation through the Saviour.

Bible reading
Matthew 24:32–51

Prayer—making sure!
In your own words, speak to the Saviour about this. Jesus longs to hear us say we trust him alone for our salvation. Will you be with 'the saved of the earth' as they gather? Because only God knows the day or the hour of his return, please make sure you will be ready!

After praying, read 1 Thessalonians 4:13–18. What comfort!

Index of hymns